Understanding the
Book of Hebrews

UNDERSTANDING THE BOOK OF HEBREWS

The Story Behind the Sermon

Kenneth Schenck

Westminster John Knox Press
LOUISVILLE • LONDON

© 2003 Kenneth L. Schenck

Translations of Greek and Latin are the author's. Scripture quotations, where indicated, are from the New Revised Standard Version of the Bible, copyright © 1989 by the Division of Christian Education of the National Council of the Churches of Christ in the U.S.A., and are used by permission.

Book design by Sharon Adams
Cover design by Lisa Buckley
Cover photograph: Papyrus roll with Epistle to the Hebrews. 3rd–4th Century, A.D.
© *Bettmann/CORBIS*

First edition
Published by Westminster John Knox Press
Louisville, Kentucky

This book is printed on acid-free paper that meets the American National Standards Institute Z39.48 standard. ♾

PRINTED IN THE UNITED STATES OF AMERICA

03 04 05 06 07 08 09 10 11 12 — 10 9 8 7 6 5 4 3 2 1

Library of Congress Cataloging-in-Publication Data

Schenck, Kenneth, 1966-
    Understanding the book of Hebrews : the story behind the sermon / Kenneth Schenck.—
1st ed.
        p. cm.
    Includes bibliographical references.
    ISBN 0-664-22428-8 (alk. paper)
    1. Bible. N. T. Hebrews—Criticism, interpretation, etc. I. Title.

BS2775.52.S34 2003
227'.8706—dc21

                                                                          2003047916

To Angela

Contents

Introduction

Imagine that you find a letter one day while you are out for a walk. No one has signed the letter, and the letter itself does not say who received it. Further, the letter provides very little specific information at all about the situation it addresses. Obviously the person who wrote it and those who received it knew the story behind the letter very well—information they left out *precisely because it was so well known to both parties!* But all you have to go on is the content of the letter itself and your knowledge of the world in general. As you read the letter, you try to "place" it against some context that seems to fit.

We are in almost exactly the same situation when it comes to the "Epistle to the Hebrews" in the New Testament.[1] This writing does not name its author or tell us the location to which it was written. It gives us allusions to a situation, but talks about it only in a vague and somewhat metaphorical kind of way. All we have to go on is the content of the letter combined with our knowledge of the first-century world.

It is difficult for most of us to leave questions like "Who wrote Hebrews?" unanswered. We constantly face the temptation to guess at the unknown, even though we often do not have sufficient information to do so. The history of Hebrews's interpretation is full of reckless guesses and unprovable hypotheses. We guess at the author or background situation and then think we have unlocked the epistle's mysteries, but the interpretations that result often have little to do with Hebrews's original meaning. The starting point is often so skewed or hypothetical that the end result carries no force at all.

The only legitimate place to start interpreting Hebrews is with what the text of Hebrews itself tells us. Studies that begin by deciding on a highly specific author, audience, or situation are bound to lead us astray. Such starting hypotheses make it hard for us to hear Hebrews with open ears. Nevertheless, Hebrews does give us some general hints about its original situation, even if we must sometimes dig deeply to find them.

For example, while we will probably never know the name of the author, we know with a great deal of certainty that it was a man[2] who belonged to Hellenistic or Greek-speaking Christianity.[3] Further, the author calls Hebrews a "word of exhortation" (Heb. 13:22). This phrase probably indicates it was a short sermon or homily that the author sent to some other destination.[4] With regard to the audience, we know that they have been Christians for some time (e.g., 5:12) and that the author is writing to reinforce their confidence (e.g., 10:35–36) in the reality of the salvation Christ has provided for them (e.g., 10:23).

Beyond some of these basics, Hebrews gives us much room for speculation.[5] But it is best to hold off as long as possible before making educated guesses about many of these issues. We want to listen to the text in as unhindered a manner as possible. For this reason, we will not speculate about the specifics of the situation that gave rise to Hebrews until the end of this book (chapter 6). The bulk of the book attempts to present the "thought world" of Hebrews— the world of its original meaning—on Hebrews's own terms (chapters 1–5).

> **Hellenistic**   Greek in culture or Greek-speaking.
>
> **homily**   A short sermon.

Similar to early Christian thought in general, Hebrews's thought is fundamentally *narrative* in orientation. In other words, the arguments of Hebrews center on a *story*, the story of how God has provided salvation to his people through Christ. We call this the story of salvation history. This simple observation holds great potential for our understanding of Hebrews and the New Testament in general.

The story orientation of the Gospels and Acts is obvious enough, since they are actually narrative in form. Accordingly, we can analyze them by breaking them down into the various events, characters, and settings that together comprise their plots. A branch of biblical studies known as narrative criticism has in fact done this with a great deal of success.[6] This method usually ignores such questions as who the author was, how the Gospels have used their sources, or even if the events of the Gospels actually took place. Instead, narrative criticism tries to read the Gospels and Acts just as you would read any story, focusing "exclusively" on the text itself rather than on issues of background and history.[7]

> **narrative**   Story, in form or nature.
>
> **salvation history**   The story of how God has brought salvation to his people.

Hebrews, on the other hand, does not "look" like a story any more than Paul's letters do. Its discourse—the way the words of its text are presented to a reader—is a sermon that makes arguments. Yet it is important to realize that *all its arguments are based on a story*. Hebrews argues about the significance of various *events* in the history of Israel as well as about the significance of Jesus' death and resurrection. Jesus is thus a *character* in the story, as are Moses, angels, and a host of other figures from the Jewish Scriptures. Even those in the audience of Hebrews itself are characters in the plot. Settings like heaven and earth also play important roles in the story. For example, Hebrews argues that Christ's sacrifice is superior because it takes place in heaven (8:1–6).

> **plot** The combination of events, characters, and settings such that they comprise a story.
>
> **narrative criticism** An approach to interpretation that "brackets" historical factors as much as possible in order to read a story as a self-contained world.
>
> **discourse** The words on the page of a text—a text as it presents itself to a reader.

These events, characters, and settings comprise the "story world" or "narrative world" of Hebrews, the story that stands behind its discourse. Realizing that such a story lies behind its arguments provides us with an appropriate entryway into the overall thought of this document.[8]

On the other hand, since the discourse of Hebrews is not a narrative, we are in a somewhat different situation than when we are analyzing the narrative world of a Gospel. In some ways, our situation is easier than when interpreting the Gospels. After all, Hebrews comes right out and tells us the significance of its various characters, events, and settings. We largely have to "read between the lines" to infer such things when we are analyzing a Gospel.

Yet the fact that the story is expressed as rhetoric—words formulated in such a way as to persuade—introduces important elements we must also consider if we are to hear Hebrews accurately. Ancient rhetoric, for example, was about far more than a *logical* argument or reasoning (the *logos* mode of rhetoric). Of equal importance were "personal" arguments (*ethos*) that convinced the audience they should trust the speaker and "emotional" arguments (*pathos*) that moved the audience primarily by way of honor and shame. Even when rhetoric is functioning in logical mode, an author can argue metaphorically or allegorically, meaning that we must decide how much is invested in each particular image or statement. Hebrews's "thought world" is thus much more than its "narrative world."[9] It is the "story-as-discoursed" in rhetoric.

> **story world** The abstracted story—with events, characters, and settings—that is evoked by a text. Such a text might be a narrative version of the story (the same story can be narrated in many different ways) or some other kind of "text," like a sermon making an argument from a story.
>
> **rhetoric** Words formulated in such a way as to persuade.

The following chapters approach the text of Hebrews with these insights in mind. Chapter 1 presents an overview of Hebrews's story world in terms of events, characters, and settings. Chapters 2 through 5 then explore that story world in greater depth, showing how the author of Hebrews has argued from it in his sermon.

For example, chapter 2 orients us to the basic goal of the story, the salvation of God's people. In particular, it investigates the crisis that gave rise to the story in the first place. While God had created humanity to experience glory and honor in the creation (e.g., 2:7–8), we do not currently experience it. Chapter 3 focuses on the rhetoric of Heb. 1. This chapter gives us a snapshot of the climax of the story—Christ's enthronement as cosmic king at God's right hand. We see the highest christological moment in the plot, the point at which Jesus receives the titles of Son of God, Christ, and Lord.

Chapter 4 discusses the various characters of the plot: individuals like Moses, the wilderness generation, and Jesus himself. Some of these served as examples for the audience to emulate, while others gave them patterns to avoid. We look at the settings of the plot and dig deeper into the Christology of Hebrews in chapter 5. It investigates the metaphor of Christ's high priesthood and explores what the author might have meant by the sacrifice and offering of Christ in a heavenly sanctuary.

Only after this in-depth consideration of Hebrews's story and rhetoric does chapter 6 speculate about the specifics of the situation that gave rise to the epistle. It starts with the more certain and moves to the speculative, suggesting which options seem most coherent with the overall study. The book concludes with an overview of Hebrews's thought that brings together the various insights we gained along the way.

Chapter 1

The Story World of Hebrews

THE BASIC PLOT

A story is made up of three basic components: the things that happen (events), those who participate in the things that happen (characters), and the times and places where those things happen (settings). The story that the Epistle to the Hebrews evokes is no different. The drama has events, characters, and settings. The only difference is that the author of Hebrews presents his[1] version of the story in the form of an argument, rather than in a narrative. He is thus able to make "the moral of the story" abundantly clear.

Before we look in more detail at the events, characters, and settings of the story from which Hebrews argues, it would be good to get a sense of the overall plot of salvation history as the author understood it. Since a person can tell the same story in several different ways, we will try to tell it in the way the author of Hebrews might have if he had written it as a play. In other words, we will try to emphasize the parts of the story he emphasizes and give less attention to the parts to which he pays less attention.

> **plot** The combination of events, characters, and settings such that they comprise a story.

Prologue

The story world of Hebrews opens with humanity already under the power of the devil (Heb. 2:14). God had intended humans to rule the creation perpetually with glory and honor (v. 7), but now death was their consistent fate.

Hebrews does not explicitly state the circumstances by which this situation

> Since the children have flesh and blood in common, he himself partook of them similarly in order that he might destroy the one who has the power of death—that is, the devil.
>
> —Heb. 2:14

came about, but it is clear that the main obstacle to their intended status is sin (2:17; 4:15). As long as their sin remains, they will die and fail to attain the glory intended by God (2:8). This problem seems to have beset humanity from its earliest days, even "from the foundation of the world" (9:26), although it was God who created the heavens and the earth (3:4).

Act I: Days of Anticipation

The principal setting is the earthly, created realm. The characters and events are numerous. People live their whole lives subject to the fear of death (2:15). There is no real atonement for their sins (10:4), but God enacts through angels a covenant that points by way of example to the solution he has planned (2:2).

This first "covenant," the law, involved the continual offering of sacrifices in an earthly sanctuary (10:1). It was God's "word" to that age, mediated by the angels (2:2) through Moses (3:5; 8:5) to God's people (1:1), but it was never intended to be the solution to humanity's problem. Rather, it was a shadowy example of what God was planning to do through Christ (8:5). Countless priests offered countless sacrifices, none of which was truly able to remove the consciousness of sins (10:2). Once a year, a high priest passed through the veil of the earthly tabernacle into the Holy of Holies with blood, a passage symbolizing that the way to true atonement was not possible until the first age passed away (9:6–9).

> For the law . . . is never able to perfect those who approach with the same sacrifices that they offer continuously. Otherwise, would the worshipers not have stopped sacrificing once they had been cleansed and had no more consciousness of sins?
>
> —Heb. 10:2–3

Those who heard God's word in this first age responded in two basic ways: Some heard the word with enduring faith and others disbelieved God's promises. Abraham serves as a prime example of someone who responded to God's word with complete faith in the unseen (11:8–10). In him we see that God does indeed keep his promises (6:15). Hebrews 11 enumerates a host of others who demonstrated a similar faith, individuals like Abel, Enoch, Noah, and Sarah. These "heroes of faith" believed in God's promise even though they died before seeing it come to pass (11:39–40).

On the other hand, the wilderness generation serves as the principal example of disbelief in God's word. Although they left Egypt with the promise of entering God's rest (4:1–2), their lack of faith resulted only in death (3:17). Esau is an even more startling example of unbelief. After losing his status as "firstborn," he was unable to regain his sonship, even though he sought a place of repentance with tears (12:16–17).

Act I ends with the coming of Jesus to the earthly realm, his earthly life, and his climactic death. Humanity's flesh and blood made them prey to death and the devil. Accordingly, Jesus also partakes of them (2:14). A body is prepared for him as he comes to substitute a new covenant in place of the old (10:5–9). In the days of his flesh he demonstrates a sinless conformity to the first covenant (4:15; 5:8). Like the patriarchs of old, he becomes a supreme example of earthly faithfulness (12:2). He prays with godly fear to the one who is able to rescue him from the grave (5:7). He was made lower than the angels for a little while, so that he might taste death for all humanity (2:9).

His death thus brings about the climactic conclusion of the first act. Hebrews understands this death metaphorically as a sacrifice, the decisive and final atonement for sins (10:14). Indeed, Hebrews thinks metaphorically of the entire movement of the story from Jesus' death to his passage through the heavens as the entrance of a heavenly high priest into a true, heavenly tabernacle (8:1–2). Now God's definitive solution to the problem of humanity can be put into effect.

Act II: The Consummation of the Ages

We can thus picture the second act of the story commencing with a celebration of the enthroned Christ as God seats him at his majestic right hand (Heb. 1). Salvation is now possible. The angels worship him as God leads him into the heavenly realm (1:6) and crowns him as royal Son (1:5), king of the coming world (2:5). He is the one through whom God creates order out of chaos, the very wisdom through which God created the heavens and earth (1:3, 10). He sits at God's right hand waiting for his enemies to be subjected (10:13), after which he will return a second time to bring the play to its conclusion (9:28). In the meantime, he serves as a heavenly intercessor for the sins of all who would approach the throne of God's grace with boldness (7:25).

As in the first age, there are two basic responses to God's consummative word. One can respond in faith or one can disbelieve. Both the eyewitnesses of the "word" spoken through Christ (2:3) and the former leaders of the audience's own community (13:7) are positive examples of endurance until the end.

The recipients of Hebrews are also a part of the story. They are characters in the second act of the drama, the time when salvation is available to those who respond with belief. The author/preacher places them on the brink of the choice that faced the wilderness generation. They have left "Egypt"; they have partaken of the Holy Spirit (6:4) and are God's children (12:7); Christ's atonement for their sins remains (10:26). Yet "today" they are faced with a choice: Will they harden their hearts as did the Israelites in the desert (4:7–11), or will they continue in faithfulness

> After he had made a cleansing for sins, he sat on the right hand of majesty in the highest places, having become as much better than the angels as the name he has inherited is more excellent than theirs.
>
> —Heb. 1:3–4

until the end (10:39)? The author is convinced that they will make the right choice (6:9).

The author knows how the current act will end, even if the audience is still writing some of its part in the drama. Christ's victorious atonement has set in motion a sequence of events that can only culminate in his return to judge the world. The righteous spirits of the perfected will be saved (12:23; 10:14), but God's consuming fire will remove the created realm. He will shake both the created heavens and earth so that only the unshakable remains (12:26–29). Those who have responded with disbelief will fall fearfully into the hands of the living God (10:31; 12:23; 4:12–13), but those who have responded with faith will finally reach their heavenly homeland (11:14), the heavenly Jerusalem (12:22). These events will bring Christ's work to a close vis-à-vis the earth but provide a new beginning for God's people.

Epilogue

As with the events at the beginning of the plot, Hebrews gives us little information about the eternity after. We know that Christ will reign as king in the coming world, as will his "brothers" (2:5). It will be an unshakable kingdom (12:28), a true rest for the people of God (4:9). Hebrews does not enumerate the story beyond this point, however; it only implies that such a kingdom is worth the endurance necessary to achieve it. Those who respond in faith have every reason to hold fast.

THE SETTINGS OF THE STORY

The settings of a story are the times and places where things happen. The *times* when things happen are called "temporal" settings, while the *places* where things happen are called "spatial" settings. In the story world of Hebrews, each one of these has certain connotations. For example, the created realm, the realm of flesh and blood, is a place where death reigns and where no fleshly sacrifice can truly take away sins. On the other hand, a spiritual "offering" in heaven can be effective not least because it is done in the right place. Settings can thus help or hinder a character from reaching his or her goal in the story.

> **settings** The times and places where things happen in a story.

Heaven and the Created Realm

Hebrews makes reference to two basic realms where things happen in the plot. The one is the created realm, consisting of the created heavens and earth. The other is the heaven where God's throne is.[2] While Hebrews does not say that the created realm is evil, this realm is clearly inferior to the heavenly realm, and its weaknesses may very well contribute to the devil's power.

The primary relationship between the heavenly and the earthly, therefore, is one of contrast. We could mention more specific settings within each of these two realms. For example, Mt. Sinai (12:18) and the wilderness tabernacle (9:1) are two specific earthly settings in the story, while the heavenly sanctuary is a heavenly setting (8:1; 9:11). It is the location of these particular places in either heaven or earth, however, that gives them their significance for the plot. Indeed, in the case of the "heavenly tabernacle" the author may not even have a distinct place in mind. We can make a good argument that the heavenly sanctuary is basically a metaphorical way of referring to heaven itself.[3]

> For if he were *on earth* he would not be a priest, since there are [already] those who offer the gifts according to the law, who serve the *heavenly* sanctuary by way of a shadowy example.
>
> —Heb. 8:4–5

Hebrews does not explicitly say why the created realm is destined for God's cataclysmic shaking (12:27), nor does it tell us why the devil holds power over humanity on earth (2:5, 15). Nevertheless, the entirety of its argument associates the created realm with the inferior and with imperfection.[4] The earthly sanctuary does not effect true atonement and cannot compare with the greater and more perfect heavenly tabernacle, which is "not of this creation" or "made with human hands" (8:1–2, 5; 9:1, 11). The heavenly Jerusalem is vastly superior to the earthly Mt. Sinai (12:18, 22). Christ's "heavenly" reign will last forever, while the created heavens and earth "will all become old like a garment" (1:11).[5] At one point the author almost implies that the creation was in need of redemption from the moment God created it (9:26).[6]

Related to the contrast between earthly and heavenly is an implied contrast between flesh and spirit.[7] The author implicitly associates humanity's problem with the fact that we currently exist in flesh. Since the children needing atonement share flesh and blood in common, Christ similarly partakes of them to defeat the one "holding the power of death" (2:14). The connection between the human body and death is of course fundamental to human experience. Therefore, for Christ to partake of flesh and blood is for him to enter the territory where the devil holds sway.

> For if the blood of goats and bulls and the ash of a heifer sprinkled on those who have become unclean sanctifies for the cleansing of the *flesh*, how much more will the blood of Christ, who through eternal *spirit* offered himself blameless to God, cleanse our consciousness of dead works so that we can serve the living God.
>
> —Heb. 9:13–14

The author interestingly refers to Christ's earthly life as "the days of his flesh" in 5:7, implying that he now has a different form of existence, namely a spiritual one.[8] When Hebrews writes of God sending Jesus to the earthly realm, the author uses a text of Ps. 40 that reads "you prepared a *body* for me" (Heb. 10:5). He uses language that highlights the relevance of Jesus' physicality for his earthly mission, as well as his far superior spiritual state of existence now.

Hebrews thus makes clear distinctions between heavenly and earthly existence. In this contrast, it not only associates the earthly with humanity's susceptibility to sin and death, but it also highlights the inability of anything earthly to bring about atonement. By contrast, the heavenly realm holds out the hope and promise of true redemption.[9]

The Former Age and These Last Days

If the plot takes place in two different spatial settings, Hebrews also pictures two basic temporal settings for the story—the former age and the age that Christ inaugurates. As the first two verses of Hebrews say, "Although God formerly spoke many times and in many ways to the fathers through the prophets, in these last days he spoke to us through a Son." These two periods of salvation's history, the former days and these last days, correspond to Act I and Act II in the drama we presented at the beginning of the chapter. They also correspond in general to the two spatial settings we have just discussed—heaven and the created realm. The principal setting of the old covenant was in the earthly realm, while the heavenly realm dominates the new.

However, *the two spatial settings overlap* in the story. God's people are still on earth even though their heavenly salvation is secured (see Fig. 1). While Christ's enthronement marks the decisive beginning of the new age, the earthly realm continues to exist in its old form, even if it is outdated and passing away (8:13). Nevertheless, the heavenly work of Christ is in force, enabling the human spirit to be sanctified (10:14; 12:23). Hebrews argues strongly that continued reliance on earthly models of atonement is not only ineffective (7:19) but also constitutes apostasy from Christ (5:11–6:6).

> Although God *formerly* spoke in many and various ways to the fathers by way of the prophets, *in these last days* he has spoken to us by way of a Son.
> —Heb. 1:1–2

The relationship between the two ages is one of promise and fulfillment. Those who are faithful in the old age realize all along that they are awaiting something in the future. "Faith is the substance of things for which one hopes" (11:1), the author says before enumerating a long list of faithful individuals from the age of the first covenant. "All of these died in faith, although they did not receive the promise. But they saw it from a distance, greeted it, and confessed that they were foreigners and aliens on the earth" (v. 13). Moses similarly was a servant God sent to witness to the things that God was *going to* speak through Christ (3:5).

Hebrews also argues strongly that God never intended the earthly sacrificial system—or "cultus," as it is sometimes called—to be the way of atonement. Rather, it was a shadowy example of the atonement Christ would truly provide

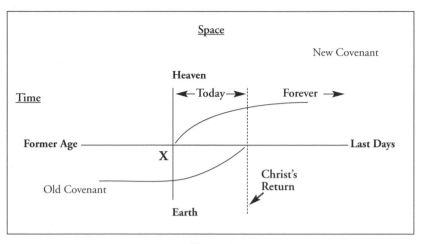

Figure 1

(8:5).[10] Hebrews 10:4 notes that "it is impossible for the blood of bulls and goats to take away sins." Yet this was the method of sacrifice that God ordained in the old covenant. It is thus clear that God never intended the old covenant cultus to be the way of true atonement. It rather was a God-ordained pointer toward that which he would eventually do through Christ.

"Today" and "Forever"

Even though Christ has effected a decisive atonement, the created realm remains, and God's people still await salvation. This situation gives rise to two further temporal settings even within the age of the new covenant. On the one hand, there is the present time during which the earthly and heavenly realms coexist uneasily. Yet Hebrews also anticipates the coming judgment that will lead to the removal of the created realm.

The Epistle to the Hebrews itself gives us words we can use to label these periods when it notes "Jesus Christ is the same yesterday, today, and forever" (13:8). "Yesterday" here evokes images of the "former days" during which the audience of Hebrews was exemplary in its faithful endurance of persecution (10:32–34). They found Christ to be faithful to them then. "Today and forever" remind the audience that Jesus remains faithful to them in their current situation and that he will be faithful to them forever.

However, if we take the verse slightly out of context, the word *today* strongly reminds us of the author's argument in Heb. 3–4. There, he speaks of "today" as every day of this present period, during which God's people must reaffirm their commitment to endure in faithfulness (3:13). If we expand

> Encourage one another every day that is called "today" so none of you will be hardened by the deceitfulness of sin.
>
> —Heb. 3:13

> ## The Settings of the Story
>
> ### I. Settings in Space
> - The Highest Heaven ("heaven itself," Heb. 9:24)
> - The Created Realm ("the things that have been made," 12:27)
>
> ### II. Settings in Time
> - The Former Age ("formerly," 1:2)
> - The Last Days ("today," 3:13)
> - The Age to Come ("forever," Heb. 13:8)

the meaning of Hebrews's terms, we might call this present period of time "today," the time between Christ's decisive sacrifice and his return. "Forever" then becomes a convenient way of referring to the remainder of eternity after the removal of the created realm.

The author of Hebrews meant for Christ's eternal faithfulness to provide confident hope to his audience.[11] "Today," they needed endurance. Hebrews skillfully alternates between teaching and exhortation to make this point. While the teaching sections build the argument of Hebrews, the exhortations consistently reinforce the need for the audience to hold fast and endure confidently in their hope.[12] "Today," the audience must choose to affirm their faith in what Christ has done, while looking forward to the "forever" God has promised. Chapter 6 will explore in more detail this situation in which the audience finds itself.

THE EVENTS OF THE STORY

The events of a story, the things that happen, form the "backbone" of a plot. They move the story from one point to the next. An event can give rise to a plot; it can change the direction of a plot; it can bring a story to a close.

> **events** The things that take place in a

Events are the dots through which a "storyline" is drawn. The author of Hebrews finds several specific events to be particularly significant in the story of salvation's history. For example, the death and exaltation of Christ are clearly the key events of the story. The author also finds certain *kinds* of events important for his argument, such as the yearly entrance of Levitical high priests into the earthly tabernacle. In each case, the significance the author finds in each event leads to the arguments he makes as he retells the story for his audience.

The Beginnings of the Story

The author of Hebrews does not discuss the beginnings of the plot with his audience. He does not say much about the creation of the world or about the events that led to the current state of humanity. Since the audience finds itself in the final moments of the story, the author is more interested in the solution to humanity's problem than in its origins. Chapter 2 will address some of these gaps in our knowledge by pushing behind Hebrews to the early Christian traditions on which the author drew.

Nevertheless, we can speak with some confidence about one or two events at the beginning of the plot. The first is, of course, God's creation of the world (2:10; 3:4; 11:3), although Hebrews also refers at least figuratively to Christ as the agent of creation (1:3, 10–12). We have already mentioned Heb. 9:26, where the author implies that the need for atonement goes back to "the foundation of the world." If we took this statement literally, we would conclude that God created the world flawed from the very beginning.

Indeed, in one reconstruction of the story's beginning, creation is God's imposition of order on already flawed matter—not creation out of nothing (*ex nihilo*). Although Christians and Jews commonly think of creation in this way today, it was a somewhat rare idea in the ancient world. Perhaps the author of Hebrews thought that the matter from which humanity was made implicitly needed redemption. We might see the final removal of the created realm as God eliminating the ultimate source of the problem.[13]

> By faith we know that the worlds were mended by the word of God, with the implication that what is visible has not come about by means of things that appear.
> —Heb. 11:3

However, it seems more likely in the light of other early Christian traditions that another event lies at the root of humanity's problem. Paul draws on some of the same biblical traditions as Hebrews (e.g., Ps. 8), and he implies that death came into the world through the sin of Adam (e.g., Rom. 5:17). Hebrews also alludes to the Wisdom of Solomon, which says that death entered the world through the devil's envy (Wis. 1:13; 2:23–24; compare Heb. 2:14).[14] These connections point us in the direction of the devil's envy and Adam's sin as culprits for the human predicament. They point us to Gen. 2–3 as the event resulting in the perversion of God's good creation.

Events of the Former Age

Several kinds of events took place repeatedly in the former age, events that paint us a good picture of what this age was like in general. For example, countless humans died owing to their sin. Sacrifices were repeatedly offered for sin, none of which actually took it away. Each and every such event pointed forward in the story to the decisive sacrifice that Christ would offer.

> Every priest has stood daily ministering and offering the same sacrifices often, which are never able to take away sins.
> —Heb. 10:11

Countless humans—those of Israel in particular—heard God's word through the prophets. Some of them mixed their hearing with faith; others did not. Hebrews 11 presents a number of faith events, each of which demonstrates the appropriate reaction to God's word. Other events, such as the faithlessness of the wilderness generation, underscore the consequences of unbelief.

> These all died in faith even though they had not received the promises, but they saw them from afar, greeted them, and confessed that they were strangers and aliens on the earth.
> —Heb. 11:13

In terms of particular events, the mediation of the law through angels is one of the most significant in the former age. Hebrews 2:2 makes mention of a "word spoken through angels" that included commands to be obeyed. In the light of parallel comments in the rest of the New Testament (Acts 7:53; Gal. 3:19), it is clear that this "word" was the law, mediated through angels to Moses.

In Hebrews, the "law" refers primarily to the Old Testament cultus.[15] The author implies in 7:11 that the foundation of the law was the Levitical priesthood and that any change in priesthood necessitated a change of law (v. 12). The mediation of the law through angels thus stands in contrast to the mediation of the new covenant through Christ, which the author believes was the institution of a new law (8:6).[16] However, God writes this "law" on the hearts of his people—that is, he forgives their sins (8:10; 10:16).

The giving of the law presents God's people with a sketch, a "parable" of what will later come through Christ (9:8–9). It holds only a "shadow" of the coming good things; it is not the "image" of those things (10:1). Its sacrifices and tabernacle only point forward to the death and victorious exaltation of Christ. In and of itself, it cannot atone.

> Moses was faithful as a servant in his [God's] house in order to witness to the things that would eventually be spoken, but Christ [was faithful] as a Son in his house.
> —Heb. 3:5–6

Christ's death does atone for sins, however, in the climactic moment of the entire story. He has come to the earthly realm and has lived a sinless life. He dies a faithful death, believing that God can raise the dead (5:7; cf. 11:12, 19, 35). In response God exalts him to his right hand (1:13), enthrones him as royal Son of God (1:5),[17] and holds out potential atonement to all humanity through him (2:10).

In Hebrews it is difficult to break down this saving moment into separate events. On the one hand, the New Testament writings in general have no problem distinguishing the event of Christ's death from his resurrection, ascension, or seating at God's right hand. However, the author of Hebrews integrates these separate events together by using them to construct a metaphor in which Christ's death is a sacrifice offered in a heavenly tabernacle on a

> In the days of his flesh he offered both petitions and supplications with strong crying and tears to the one able to save him out of death, and he was heard because of his godly fear.
> —Heb. 5:7

decisive "Day of Atonement." The whole movement from Christ's death to his "session," or seating, at God's right hand thus functions somewhat as a single event in the plot.

When Hebrews speaks of Christ as a high priest who enters a heavenly taber-nacle (8:1–2) to offer his blood (9:12), the author is not thinking of a literal struc-ture in heaven, nor does he believe that Christ literally brought blood to the right hand of God. Christ's death *is* an atoning sacrifice for sins[18] and Christ *does* pass through the heavens to the throne of God (4:14), but it is on a metaphorical level that the author understands this sequence of events to be the slaughter of an ani-mal that is brought through a sanctuary into a heavenly Holy of Holies. The imagery breaks down at several points if taken too literally.[19] References to this metaphorical event are thus a complex, yet relevant way for the author to argue that Christ's death is an efficacious atonement for sins. Hebrews claims that what Christ did has replaced the Levitical cultus in its entirety.

Events in the Age of Christ

We begin Act II of the plot with a celebration in heaven as Christ is victoriously seated at God's right hand. He has accomplished salvation; he is triumphantly enthroned as Son of God. The chain of Old Testament citations in Heb. 1:5–14 read like an enthronement ceremony, a hymnic celebration of Christ's seating at God's right hand.[20]

It is easy enough to see why some disagree with this interpretation. For exam-ple, Heb. 1:6 sounds to us like the worship of Christ by angels as he arrives *on earth*, not in heaven. Nevertheless, G. B. Caird presented the key to unlocking Heb. 1 when he pointed out its relation to the quotation of Ps. 8 in Heb. 2.[21] Christ was made lower than the angels *for a little while* when he was on earth, but he is now crowned with glory and honor at God's right hand.[22]

For at least two reasons, Heb. 1 makes sense as a part of the epistle's overall contrast between the old and new covenants. On the one hand, the author associates angels with the mediation and administration of the old covenant (cf. 1:14). On the other, the exaltation of Christ above the angels indicates that he has paved the way for his "brothers" also to come to glory in fulfillment of Ps. 8 (Heb. 2:10). The contrast of Heb. 1 is thus an appropriate

> Are they [angels] not all ministering spirits sent to serve because of those about to inherit salvation?
> —Heb. 1:14

beginning for a sermon holding out Christ as the solution to humanity's prob-lem. It pictures an event of celebration in which Christ is enthroned as king, wait-ing for all things to be put under his feet (2:8; 10:13) as his servants bow in obeisance (1:6).

If the second act begins with an event of celebration, it ends with an event of salvation and judgment. As with the beginning of the plot, the epistle does not

> While his voice then shook the earth, now it is promised that "yet once more I will shake not only the earth but also the heaven." The "yet once more" indicates the removal of what is shaken, as of the things that have been created, so that what is unshakable might remain.
>
> —Heb. 12:26–27

go into great detail about this event. Hebrews speaks of God's judgment in terms of fire (12:29) and the "shaking" of the created realm (12:27). It makes only one or two allusions to the fate of those who have never had faith (6:2), however, and it is not completely clear about whether the created realm is transformed or removed altogether. In general, its warnings are directed at those among God's people who might "sell their birthright" (12:16) rather than those who have never believed. Yet surely those who have never "partaken of the heavenly gift" will face God's judgment just as assuredly as those who turn away from Christ after believing.

Hebrews uses a number of images in reference to salvation. It is the "coming world" (2:5), "glory" (2:10), a "Sabbath rest" (4:9), "the promise" (6:12; 10:36), "things hoped for" (11:1), a heavenly city and homeland (11:14–16), Zion and the heavenly Jerusalem (12:22), and "an unshakable kingdom" (12:28). When Christ comes a second time, salvation will come for those who have held firm until the end (3:14; 9:28).

Before this final event, the audience of Hebrews faces an event in its own life. It is the choice that they are currently facing. Will they take the path of faithfulness, a way trodden by countless examples of faith, or will they take the way of apostasy as Esau and the wilderness generation? "Today" is a time when the audience must decide whether to "enter God's rest" and continue toward the promised land or to fall away. The author is convinced that they will make the right choice.

Events in the Story

I. **The Beginnings of the Plot**
- The creation of the world (Heb. 11:3)
- The origins of the problem (Adam, 2:8; the devil, 2:14)

II. **Events of the Former Age**
- Countless human deaths (2:15)
- Responses of faith and disobedience to God's word of promise (3:19; 11:13)
- The mediation/administration of the law (2:2; 3:5)
- Continuous offering of sacrifices (10:11)
- The faithful earthly life of Jesus (5:7–8)

III. **Events in the Age of Christ**
- The high priestly offering of Christ (9:27–28)
- The enthronement of Christ as cosmic king (1:3–4)
- Responses of faith and disobedience to God's word of salvation (2:3)
- The situation of the audience of Hebrews (10:26–39)
- The administration of judgment/salvation to the created realm (12:25–29)

THE CHARACTERS IN THE STORY

The characters of a story are those who participate in the things that happen. From the standpoint of plot, the most significant characters are those who move it along. For example, since every story involves a goal of some kind, some characters help the plot move toward reaching that goal (helpers) while others put obstacles in the way of its achievement (opponents). In Hebrews, God is an essential character because he starts the story, while Christ is essential because he brings about the story's goal, salvation. On the other hand, the devil is the main opponent to the goal.

Not all characters in a story move the plot forward. Some clarify the overall problems and goals of the plot. Some participate in the story without clearly impacting its movement toward a final outcome. Humanity's role in the story of salvation history is of this sort. We experience death and may enjoy the benefit of salvation, but we do not move the plot from one point to the next.[23]

Further, the type of character called a "foil" is only in the story to teach us about a more significant character. Foils do not move a story along. Melchizedek plays this kind of role in the story world of Hebrews. The author is interested in Melchizedek only for what he might teach us about Christ as a priest, not because he is interested in Melchizedek per se.

God

The most important character in the plot of salvation history is, of course, God. In a sense, he is the true "author" and initiator of the story. He is the one "for whom" and "through whom" everything exists (2:10). The plot moves at his bidding. He is not only the creator (3:4) but also the one who "has spoken" decisively in both acts of the drama (1:1–2). As judge of all things, he will bring the story to its final conclusion when he "shakes" and removes the created realm (12:23, 25–29).

Hebrews makes at least four clear affirmations that God is the ultimate creator of the world. Hebrews 3:4 states that he is the one "who has built all things," and 2:10 notes that he is the one "through whom" all things exist. Hebrews 11:3 notes that the worlds were formed by the word (*rema*) of God. Even Heb. 1:3, which seems to speak of Christ as the agent of creation, affirms that it was God who was making the worlds *through* Christ.[24] One must therefore read Heb. 1:10–12 very carefully. Even though these verses appear to describe Christ as the creator of the heavens and earth, the verses may be saying something subtler about Christ as the one God has used to create order in his creation out of chaos.[25]

Within the created realm, God is clearly the "speaker" of both salvation and judgment for the world and all in it. The Epistle to the Hebrews abounds with word and "speaking" imagery, language that the author uses to indicate God's involvement in his creation.[26] For the author of Hebrews, the ultimate background against which to understand this language is probably the Jewish Scriptures in passages such as Gen. 1. "And God said, 'Let there be light.' And there was light" (Gen. 1:3). God speaks and it is done. No word of God ever fails to accomplish its task (Isa. 55:11).[27]

God speaks often in the story, and his word is decisive in each case. On the one hand, he speaks words of salvation for his people. In the former age, he spoke words of promise through the prophets (Heb. 1:1). He also spoke the law through the mediation of angels (2:2). In these last days, God began to speak a word of salvation through Christ, a word passed on by those who first heard him (v. 3). It is God's speaking that installs Christ as both royal Son (1:5) and heavenly high priest (5:6), just as a previous "word" assigned angels the role of ministers in the earthly realm (1:7). Occasionally, God guarantees his words of salvation with oaths, emphasizing their surety (6:13–18; 7:20–21).

> Our God is a devouring fire.
>
> —Heb. 12:29

God's words can also speak judgment. He can make oaths that ensure the destruction of the faithless rather than their salvation (3:11; 4:3). "The *word* of God is living and active and sharper than any two-edged sword," the author says (4:12). "Everything is naked and exposed to the eyes of him whose *word* is for us" (4:13).[28] This "voice" already "shook the earth" in judgment once (12:26). When he speaks again, it will shake the entirety of the created realm.

Speakers of God's Former Words

We have just mentioned the two main ways God spoke in the former age: through prophets and angels. Since the role of angels in the story is one of the main concerns of this book's third chapter, we can simply note here that the author of Hebrews primarily relegates their significance in the story to Act I. Here they serve as messengers and servants to God's people while they are still on the earth. Not only did they mediate the law, but Heb. 1 describes them as "ministering spirits sent on behalf of those who are about to inherit salvation" (v. 14). Since God's people are "those about to inherit salvation," the primary role of angels in the story clearly relates to the earthly realm. In contrast, the coming world will not be subject to them (2:5), although they clearly participate in the worship of God and his Son in Act II (1:6; 12:22). The contrast of Christ with the angels is thus part of the contrast between the two ages and their respective covenants.

> If the word spoken through angels was sure and every transgression and act of disobedience received its just punishment, how will we escape if we neglect such a great salvation?
>
> —Heb. 2:2–3

Apart from Heb. 1:1, the epistle says little explicitly about the many and various words God spoke formerly through the prophets, but we can infer that the author is primarily thinking of the "Old" Testament. Hebrews has more allusions and quotations of the Old Testament than any other New Testament book. The author clearly considered every Scripture he used as one of God's words that came through the prophets in the former age.

Of these prophets, the author singles out Moses in significance. Yet given the incredible reverence given to Moses in this period, the role Hebrews assigns him comes off as faint praise. Aside from the faithful character of his life (11:24–29), Hebrews considers Moses' significance to lie in his testimony to what God was planning to do through Christ (3:5). For example, when God revealed the construction details of the earthly sanctuary, he was simply pointing ahead through Moses to the true tabernacle in which Christ would serve (8:5). Just as the angels were ministering spirits of the first age, Moses was also a servant in the household of God in that period (3:5). Christ is a son (3:6), however, and he inaugurates the age of sons. He shows the true significance of the "words" spoken through Moses and the angels as he fulfills the words spoken through the prophets.

Earthly Priests and High Priests

Since God never intended to take away sins through the earthly cultus, the earthly priests and high priests were simply shadowy illustrations of what Christ truly brought to pass. The law prescribes numerous types of sacrificial acts for them to perform in a number of different situations, yet all of these correspond to the one sacrifice of Christ. While they are constantly in need of replacement due to death, Christ's priestly office lasts forever. In this sense Hebrews treats the earthly priests as foils against which the identity of Christ is developed. Their value for Hebrews's argument lies in the light they shed on Christ.

> On the one hand, those who have become priests are many because death prevents them from remaining, but he [Christ] has an indestructible priesthood because he remains forever.
>
> —Heb. 7:23–24

Hebrews 7 deals extensively with the question of Christ's priestly qualifications in contrast to those of the Levitical priests. Like humanity in general, these priests cannot overcome sin or death. They must offer sacrifices for their own sins as well as for the sins of the people (5:3). They are unable to continue in their office permanently, since they eventually die (7:23).

In contrast, Christ's priesthood is based upon an "indestructible life" (7:16). He lives forever to intercede eternally for the sins of those depending on him (v. 25). Finally, the sacrifices of the earthly priests are made in the earthly realm and are thus unable to atone for sins (8:4–5). They are fit for the washing of the flesh (9:10) but not of the conscience (9:9, 14). Christ's death, on the other hand, truly takes away sin.

Those Who Persist in Faithfulness

Chapter 4 of this book will deal with the way in which Hebrews uses examples of both faith and disbelief in order to challenge its audience to be faithful, but we can briefly introduce this aspect of Hebrews now. For example, Abraham is a very important "type" or example of one who hears God's word of promise with faith. Like the recipients of the epistle, he left his previous "nationality" for a land of promise. In the meantime, he lived as a foreigner and stranger on the earth, looking forward to a heavenly city (11:9, 13). He believed in God, even though he never saw God's greatest promise come to pass (v. 13).

> Since we have such a great cloud of witnesses, let us run the race before us with endurance, laying aside every weight and the sin that easily overcomes us.
> —Heb. 12:1

Hebrews 11 presents a long list of similar faith examples, a "cloud of witnesses" to urge the audience on in their contest (12:1–2). The author commends many of these for their choice to be faithful despite the persecution and shame they faced. Abel dies, but death was not his final word (11:4). Moses chooses to subject himself to the mistreatment of God's people rather than enjoy the passing pleasures of sin (vv. 24–26). Some heroes of faith chose to be tortured rather than released, since they looked forward to a better resurrection.[29] Abraham has faith for Isaac in that, though he is about to be killed, God will make it possible for his life to continue. Of all these, Jesus provides us with the consummate example of one who endures shame and dies in faith, believing that God can raise him from the dead (5:7).

Hebrews 11 also provides us with examples of faith in God's promises at times when their fulfillment was far from obvious. The faith of these individuals was "the proof of things that are not currently visible" (v. 1). Noah built an ark before any rain was in sight (v. 7). Joseph spoke of the exodus even before the time of Israel's persecution (v. 22). These examples reinforce the author's desire for the audience to endure in faith despite how things appear.

Finally, the age of the new covenant also provides us with examples of faith. Not only did the eyewitnesses of Christ faithfully pass on the "word of salvation" (2:3), but the former leaders of the audience's own community ended on an exemplary note (13:7). The author even draws on the faithfulness of the audience itself to encourage them, reminding them how they acted during a time of earlier persecution (10:33–34). All these examples reinforce the author's central exhortation: Hang on in faithfulness to what God has done through Christ, even when such faith leads to persecution and shame.

Those Who Ultimately Disbelieve

If Abraham is an important illustration of how to have faith in the unseen, the wilderness generation is the supreme example of responding in disbelief to God's word (3:7–19). Like Abraham, they started out on a journey toward the promised land, but unlike him they failed to reach it because of unbelief. If Abraham represents the benefits of enduring till one enters the land, then the wilderness generation's fate emphasizes the peril of unbelief. Their corpses fall in the desert (v. 17). They represent those who do not hold onto the faith they had at the beginning (v. 14).

Esau is another example of a godless person. He started out as the firstborn, a son, yet he threw away his inheritance for food. Later he could not regain his sonship, even though he sought a place of repentance with tears (12:15–17). Here is perhaps the starkest challenges the author makes to his audience.

> Watch that . . . no one be sexually immoral or godless like Esau, who sold his birthright for one meal. Know that he was rejected afterward when he wanted to inherit the blessing. He did not find a place of repentance even though he looked for it with tears.
>
> —Heb. 12:16–17

Christ

Christ, of course, is the hero of the story. Through God's initiative, he brings about the decisive turning point to the plot. Faithful in the days of his flesh, he became a high priest after the order of Melchizedek and atoned for the sins of God's people. Therefore, God has enthroned him as the royal Son of God, the very embodiment of the wisdom God used in creation. Christ waits for his enemies to be put under his feet, at which point he will return a second time to save all those who have been perfected through his sacrifice.

We already mentioned that the earthly Jesus is the greatest example of responding to God's word in faith. He lives his whole life without sin, although he was tested just as his fellow humans (4:15). Although he was a son, he learned obedience through the things that he suffered (5:8). He prays to the one who is able to save him from the grave and is heard because of his godly reverence (v. 7).[30] Jesus is thus the paramount witness to faithfulness, the model example of all who would despise earthly shame as they look to the invisible (12:2; 13:12–13).

Hebrews 5:5–6 reads like Christ's resume beyond his earthly life. In verse 5 we are reminded of Christ's "appointment" by God as royal Son, a fact the author has already discussed in Heb. 1. God places him in a position of lordship over all things as he seats him at his right hand.[31] As we will see further in chapters 3 and 5 of this book, this is language of enthronement, with Christ now in a position of glory and honor, destined to rule with all things under his feet.

Hebrews 5:6 continues with another office Christ holds: that of high priest. This language is part of the epistle's high priestly metaphor and is used to pit the atoning value of Christ's death against the entirety of the old covenant cultus. In the metaphor, Christ's appointment as high priest also occurs at the point of his death and exaltation. He becomes a source of eternal salvation because he has been made perfect through sufferings (v. 9). Since his life is indestructible, he is a priest after the order of Melchizedek (5:10; 7:16).[32]

> Such a great high priest was appropriate for us: holy, without evil, blameless, having been set apart from sinners and made higher than the heavens.
>
> —Heb. 7:26

Both "appointments" are based on psalm texts in which God is thought to address the Messiah. Psalm 2:8, quoted in Heb. 5:5, reads, "You are my Son; today I have given birth to you," while Ps. 110:4, cited in Heb. 5:6, says, "You are a priest forever after the order of Melchizedek." Son and high priest would thus seem to be the two primary categories in which the author places Christ. Christ's Sonship refers primarily to his office as Lord over all things, while his high priesthood is largely a metaphor for the fact that his death atones for all and provides a way of entrance to the throne of God.

Hebrews does not directly associate Christ with the coming judgment. Instead, God is portrayed as the judge of all (10:30–31; 12:23, 29). It is salvation that Christ brings at this point of the story for those waiting for him (9:28). Beyond that point in the story we know that his enemies will finally be placed under his feet (10:13), and he will reign over the coming world (2:5).

> Remember earlier days when, after you had been enlightened, you weathered a great contest of sufferings, sometimes being publicly exposed to shame and hardships and at other times sharing those of others treated that way.
> —Heb. 10:32–33

Characters in the Story

I. Characters from the Beginnings of the Story
- God (Heb. 1:1)
- [Adam] (2:8)
- The devil (2:14)

II. Characters from the Former Age
- Speakers of God's word (angels, 2:2; Moses, 3:5; prophets, 1:1)
- Levitical priests (7:11)
- Examples of disbelief (Esau, 12:16–17; wilderness generation, 3:7–19)
- Examples of faith (cloud of witnesses, Heb. 11)

III. Characters from the Age of Christ
- Christ (Heb. 1–13)
- Former leaders of the community/faith (13:7)
- The author and audience themselves

The Audience of Hebrews

We have already mentioned several aspects of the audience of Hebrews as characters in the plot. For example, the author thought they had been exemplary during a previous crisis. He encourages them to "remember earlier days" when they gladly endured the shame of Christ and the plundering of their possessions (10:32).

They have thus been Christians for some time when Hebrews is written. They are "partakers" of the Christ (3:14) and have been enlightened. They are partakers of the Holy Spirit (6:4), and the sacrifice of Christ remains in effect for them (10:26). Yet the author calls them "hard of hearing" (5:11) and says that they need to be retaught the basics of Christianity. While they should be teachers by this time, they still need baby's milk (v. 12).

The recurring exhortations to endure indicate clearly that the author is concerned that the community hold fast to their profession of faith. They have started out on the journey of faith, but the author does not wish their corpses to fall in the desert, short of the land of promise. He wishes them to be like Abraham and the cloud of witnesses who died in faith even though the promise had not yet arrived.

If the author's expositions are relevant at

all to these exhortations, we must also conclude that the audience is tempted to rely inappropriately in some way on old covenant means of atonement. Interestingly, however, the author never concludes his arguments with a statement like, "Don't rely on the Levitical system." Rather, he begins and ends his main argument with a plea for them to have boldness and confidence in the atoning value of Christ's death. Perhaps under pressure of some kind from their environment, their confidence in Christ's atonement is wavering. Reliance on Levitical means of atonement is the most tempting alternative to Christ but probably not the focus of the problem that led to the writing of Hebrews. Chapter 6 will probe these unknowns in much more depth.

CONCLUSION

The Epistle to the Hebrews is not a narrative. It is a sermon sent to a community of faith in order to challenge them to reaffirm values and beliefs they have previously held about Christ. The author/preacher hopes that their faithfulness to God's word through Christ will return to its former vigor and boldness.

Yet even if Hebrews does not have the form of a narrative, it makes its arguments on the basis of a story the author and his audience hold in common. It is the story of salvation's history, with events, characters, and settings. If the author had written it as a play, he might have set the drama in two acts, setting Act I in the earthly realm where death reigns over humanity and no earthly sacrifice can truly atone.

God does not allow the story to end there, but he finds it fitting to bring about salvation through the suffering and death of Christ. Christ partakes of flesh and blood and lives a sinless life. He dies in exemplary faithfulness to God and comes forth from the dead. Exalted as God's Son, he stands in waiting to rule over all things, a heavenly high priest whose sacrifice definitively takes away sin. He will come a second time to rescue the faithful. Here is the final resolution of the plot, the completion of the work begun in Christ's sacrifice.

From this story the author argues for faithfulness on the part of his audience. They have started the journey toward a heavenly home. They have left Ur and Egypt. Will they follow the witness of the many positive examples of faith, who believed in God's promises even though they died before they came to pass? The other path leads to the judgment of God's consuming fire.

Chapter 2

Humanity's Problem and Christ's Solution

INTRODUCTION

Every story has to begin somewhere. Sometimes stories start at the beginning: We see the initial events that play themselves out in the rest of the plot. Sometimes they begin in the middle to catch our attention and then flash back to let us see how we got to that point. In some stories, we get only the barest hints about the beginnings of the plot; we only see the results as they play themselves out. In the classic tale of Cinderella, we are not told the details of her parents' deaths or about how Cinderella came to be in such dire circumstances. The plot assumes that such things have happened—they are just not a major part of the story as we usually tell it.

The story of humanity as it is "told" in some of the New Testament, chiefly in Paul's writings, is much like the Cinderella story. Only occasionally do we get the kind of hints we would like to have about the beginnings of the plot. For Paul especially, we know that humanity has a problem, a sin problem that separates us from God. We need reconciliation but are helpless to bring it about ourselves. We know far more about the solution to the problem, however, than about how the problem started.

Paul does give us some hints about the origins of the plot, hints that point in similar directions to those Hebrews gives us.[1] We find out that the problem goes back at least to the father of the human family, a man named Adam. In some way that Paul does not fully tell us, the sin of this man brought sin and death on humanity. Paul does not ask questions like what would have happened if Adam had not sinned; rather, his thinking assumes Adam's sin and the current sinfulness of a humanity that has fallen short of the glory God intended for them (Rom. 3:23).

Hebrews also leaves out many things we would like to know about the beginning of the plot. The epistle does not mention Adam, although its argument at some points comes close enough to Paul that Adam may be the culprit once again. On the other hand, Hebrews sheds light on parts of the story that Paul himself does not discuss in detail. Humanity was intended to have glory and honor, presumably to rule the earth. However, because of Adam's sin, we do not currently enjoy this privileged position. As in Paul's theology, Christ is God's solution for our problem.

HUMANITY'S PROBLEM: THE PROLOGUE OF THE STORY

Structuralism is an approach to literature that analyzes all stories in terms of the same basic pattern or structure. According to this theory, every story arises because of an unreached goal—which at times is very abstract indeed. A plot is thus the movement of a story toward that goal, although some stories end without the goal being reached.[2]

While it would not be helpful to go very deeply into the theory of structuralism, its basic approach is helpful in the way it captures the overall dynamics of a story. According to Hebrews, God created humanity to have a position of glory in the created realm, a goal now consistently frustrated by sin and death. Christ, the hero of our story, overcomes death and the devil, making it possible for us to attain the glory for which God originally intended us. Hebrews 2:5–18 presents us with an overview of these basic dynamics of the plot.

A structuralist might diagram the beginnings of Hebrews's plot in the following way[3]:

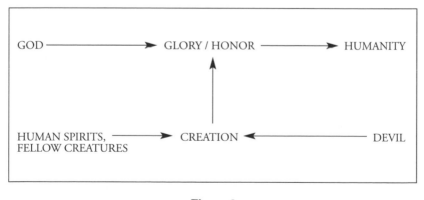

Figure 2

The "goal" of Hebrews's plot is to get glory and honor to humanity. God created the world with the intent that humans would have such an exalted status; that is, the *creation* should have brought glory and honor to humanity.[4] It is the sphere we were originally meant to rule. We remember from Gen. 1 that God not only created humans to rule over all creatures, but he also commanded humanity to "subdue" the earth itself (Gen. 1:28). In that sense, you might say that the earth's creatures were meant to "help" us achieve glory. God also "built" our spirits (and bodies?) to experience immortality rather than death.

Unfortunately, if humanity had these things going in its favor, it also had the devil as its opponent. In ways Hebrews does not enumerate, the devil managed to get power over humanity through sin—a fact that now results consistently in death for all flesh. The initial goal, getting glory to humanity, was thus foiled, giving rise to the plot. Because of sin, humans experience shame rather than glory, death rather than eternal life. These are the problems that Christ will overcome.

God's Intention to Give Glory to Humanity

In Heb. 2, the author presents an overview of how God made salvation possible for humanity through Christ. The basic gist is that God is now leading many to glory through the sufferings Christ underwent (Heb. 2:10). The author implies that Christ's death was an atoning sacrifice for sins (v. 17). The devil's power over death was the major obstacle Christ took on flesh to overcome (v. 15). Now Christ is in the process of fulfilling the words of Ps. 8 (Heb. 2:6–8), words that ascribe to him the kingship of the coming world (v. 5).

Psalm 8:4–6 reads,

> What is man that you remember him,
>   Or the son of man that you look on him?
> You made him lower than the angels for a little while;
>   You crowned him with glory and honor;
> You subjected everything under his feet.

While all scholars agree that these words in Hebrews relate to Christ in some way, not all agree that the author also believed these words to apply to humanity as well.[5] Since Heb. 1 contrasts the angels with Christ, it makes sense that Heb. 2:5 is also thinking about Christ when it says, "For God has not subjected to angels the coming world about which we are speaking." Since the author quotes Ps. 8 to back up this claim, it is reasonable to conclude that he is thinking about Christ as he quotes the psalm.

Even after he quotes Ps. 8, the author immediately points out that *Christ* is in the process of fulfilling its words (Heb. 2:9). For example, he has already been crowned with glory and honor—God exalted him after his saving death. Yet Christ is still waiting for his enemies to be put under his feet so he can return a second time (2:8; 9:28; 10:13). When we realize that Paul also quotes this psalm in reference to Christ (e.g., 1 Cor. 15:27), we understand why many scholars think it refers exclusively to him in Hebrews. In fact, the phrase "son of man," which appears in the psalm (Heb. 2:6), is one of the main titles Jesus has in the Gospels.[6]

Yet the real force of Hebrews's argument does not come through unless we realize that the psalm is not *only* about Christ. The entire reason Christ is fulfilling this psalm is because humanity was not able to do so on its own. Christ fulfills it *for* us, so that it can finally become true of us as well.

First of all, Heb. 2 not only associates the elements of this psalm with Christ; it also associates them with humanity. In fact, the most obvious reading of the psalm takes it in relation to humanity's position in the created realm—actually the original meaning of the psalm. The opening line questions why God pays attention to "man," whom God clearly created "lower than the angels." Of course, New Testament authors frequently did not interpret the Jewish Scriptures in terms of their original meaning, so we cannot automatically assume that humanity even entered the author's mind as he read the psalm.

Yet the author goes on to tell how God's purpose behind Christ's death was to *bring many sons to glory* (Heb. 2:10). In other words, Hebrews clearly associates one of the most distinctive elements of the psalm with humanity as well as Christ. The author notes that Christ and the other sons are "brothers," that "both the one that makes holy and those being made holy are of the same [sort]" (v. 11). Throughout Heb. 2 the author closely associates Christ and humanity at almost every point. It is only as a human that Christ can fulfill the psalm, and he is fulfilling it for humanity. It is a psalm about humanity that becomes true of Christ as humanity's representative.

Because the children share flesh and blood, he similarly partakes of them (2:14). He is not helping angels by assuming their identity and form; he is helping the "seed of Abraham" by becoming human (v. 16).[7] Even the verses that refer to Christ's fulfillment of the psalm have humanity in view at every step. Because of his sinless life, he is crowned with glory and honor in death, the purpose of which is that he might taste death on behalf of the "sons." As a result they too can attain glory (vv. 9–10).

Even the wording of Heb. 2:8–9 reads like the unfolding of a plot. The psalm about humanity speaks of all things in subjection, but we do not see everything subjected (v. 8). Cleverly, the author words this statement in a way that does not specify the one to whom everything should be subjected. The psalm by itself would imply a reference to "man" at this point. As such, the psalm is unfulfilled. God promised a glory humanity does not have.

The order of the Greek words in the next verse suspensefully unfolds the components of the psalm again: "But the one, for a little while, being made lower than the angels, we do see...." The use of the word *but* leads us to believe that what the author is about to say will contrast with the problematic state he has just presented. His order recounts the components of the psalm one by one, climactically leading up to a human for whom some of the remaining elements of the psalm *have* become true: *Jesus*. The author goes on, "who because of the suffering of death has been crowned with glory and honor so that by the grace of God he might taste death for everyone" (2:9). The last clause confirms emphatically that the author has had humanity's problem in view all along. Christ fulfills the psalm for us so that we can also receive our promised glory. If the psalm is not understood in reference both to humanity and Christ, the final comment about what Christ has done for us becomes tangential to the train of thought.

A closer look at the way Paul himself uses Ps. 8 shows that we would also misunderstand him if we thought his use of the psalm referred only to Christ. Paul considers this psalm to be true of Christ as a counterpart to the father of the human race, Adam. Implicit in Paul's argument in 1 Cor. 15 and Rom. 5 is the idea that God originally intended this psalm to be true of Adam. In Paul's thought, humanity should have had the glory of the psalm from the very beginning, but "all have sinned and are lacking the glory of God" (Rom. 3:23). Christ thus fulfills the psalm as a "last Adam" who enables humanity to inherit its intended glory (1 Cor. 15:45). Understanding Ps. 8 to refer both to Christ and humanity thus makes the most sense of the inner logic and the overall train of thought of Heb. 2.

The Devil's Enslavement of Humanity

If the overall goal of the plot is for God to bring glory and honor to humanity, Hebrews points to death and the devil as the ultimate obstacles to the accomplishment of this goal. Here is one of the points where Hebrews is not very clear about the story. It does not give us the specifics of how the devil has kept humanity from achieving the glory God intended. Knowing the answer to this question would help us understand how Christ's sufferings enable the accomplishment of the goal.

Hebrews 2:14–15 states that Christ took on flesh and blood so that he could destroy the one holding the power of death, the devil. In so doing he would transform enslaved humanity and set them free. In this argument the author seems to connect the devil's power with human flesh and blood, for Christ must take a *body* like humanity before he can destroy this power. Indeed, Heb. 10:5 and 10 highlight the fact that God prepared a *body* for Christ so he could come to earth and save us. These verses imply that our physicality itself lies at the heart of the devil's strength over us. After all, it is our bodies that are susceptible to death in the first place.

These brief comments in Heb. 2 offer us some hints about how the devil has prevented humanity from attaining its intended glory. The thought of Hebrews is dominated by a contrast between heaven and earth. This contrast plays itself out with regard to humanity as a contrast between our bodies and our minds/spirits. For example, while the Old Testament speaks of an earthly sanctuary (9:1), Christ entered into a "greater and more perfect" (v. 11) one in heaven itself (v. 24). While God will one day "shake" the created realm—it is changing and unstable (1:11–12; 12:27)—heaven itself promises an "unshakable kingdom" (12:28). The blood of bulls and goats may clean one's *flesh* (9:13), but Christ cleanses our *conscience* by offering his eternal *spirit* to God (v. 14).[8]

Because of statements like these, many scholars have suggested that the author of Hebrews had come under the influence of Platonic thought, in particular a philosophical tradition known as Middle Platonism. Middle Platonism drew on several other philosophical traditions, including Stoicism. As the Jewish thinker Philo might have put it, this earthly world of bodies is only a shadowy version of the real, heavenly world, where we find the patterns of things on the earth. That heavenly realm is the world of spirit and mind, not to mention non-embodied spirits like angels. Even further behind/above these heavenly patterns is God, the ultimate pattern behind everything. But since God did not create the material behind the earthly realm—he just put its previously chaotic state into order—he is not responsible for the evil that plagues it.[9]

While the differences between Hebrews and Philo are extensive, they probably share some similar perspectives on the world (see Fig. 3). Hebrews actually seems to allude to the Wisdom of Solomon, a book influenced by some of the same Platonic traditions as Philo (see Fig. 4). Also like Philo, its author was probably a Jew from the Egyptian city of Alexandria. We can make a good case that all three authors came from the same general background in Greek-speaking Judaism and that, at least in some respects, they shared a similar view of the world.

One point at which both Wisdom and Hebrews seem to echo similar traditions is when they connect the devil with human death. We have already mentioned Heb. 2:14, which indicates that the devil holds power over death and thus over all humans. Wisdom 2:23–24 states similarly, "God created man for incorruption and made him in the image of his own eternity, but death entered into the world because of the devil's envy." At this point the book of Wisdom seems to be echoing the story of Gen. 2–3, where death is the consequence of the sins of Adam and Eve in the Garden of Eden.[10] In that story, a serpent tricks the first woman, Eve, into disobeying God. In the book of Wisdom, this serpent is the devil.[11] Another Jewish writing from roughly the same period may shed light on the reason for the devil's envy. In the *Life of Adam and Eve*, God commands his angels to bow before Adam because he is made in God's image. The devil refuses

> **Middle Platonism** A philosophical tradition that developed from the merging of Platonic and Stoic ideas in the late first century B.C.E. Like Middle Stoicism, it held that the human spirit derived from the divine Word or *logos* that directed the world. Like Platonism, it believed that the material world was a copy of heavenly patterns, which it equated with the Stoic *logos*.
>
> **Philo** A Jewish interpreter of the Hebrew Scriptures who lived in the Egyptian city of Alexandria during the time of Christ. He drew heavily on Middle Platonic categories for his interpretations.

> **Wisdom of Solomon** A book of wisdom reputed to come from Solomon, written in Alexandria either the first century before or after Christ. It reflects the influence of Middle Platonism at various points.
>
> **Life of Adam and Eve** Known mainly from its later Christian form, an earlier Hebrew version may have dated from the first century C.E. It imaginatively fills in missing details from the Genesis story of Adam and Eve's "fall."

Hebrews and Philo of Alexandria

While the similarities between Hebrews and Philo have often been exaggerated, they are significant enough to conclude that Philo and the author of Hebrews come from common backgrounds:

- Both were likely Greek-speaking Jews. (Philo certainly was. The author of Hebrews exclusively uses the Greek Old Testament and probably did not know Aramaic or Hebrew.)
- Both likely received a Hellenistic education, which also probably indicates that both came from the upper stratum of society. (Philo certainly did. Hebrews shows significant signs of rhetorical training and alludes to the stages of Greek education in 5:11–14.)
- Hebrews quotes the Old Testament in ways that are unique to himself and Philo, such as the way he splices Josh. 1:5 with Deut. 31:8 in Heb. 13:5 (cf. in Philo, *Conf.*, 166).
- Hebrews uses quasi-Platonic language (e.g., 1:3; 8:5; 9:23; 10:1) and is permeated by a contrast between the heavenly and the earthly that resembles Middle Platonic categories. Both employ *logos* imagery (e.g., Heb. 1:3; 4:12; *logos* language permeates Philo's writings).
- Hebrews seems to have a somewhat dualistic view of a person as body and spirit/soul/mind (cf. 9:13–14; 10:22). Philo definitely does.
- Similar conceptions of the role of angels as mediators to the earth and of the Jewish law (cf. in Philo, *Somn.* 1.141–43; *Decal.* 46).

The differences between Philo and Hebrews, on the other hand, are quite significant as well:

- Hebrews is oriented around time more than space. The idea that a saving event might take place in the ideal realm is foreign to Philo.
- Hebrews does a poor job if it intends to feature Middle Platonic categories. It chooses the more neutral word "type" from Exod. 25:40 when the explicitly Platonic term "pattern" was available in Exod. 25:9, and uses the word *upodeigma* in Heb. 8:5 (usually mistranslated "copy") rather than any of the many terms that would have capitalized on Platonic categories.
- Philo strongly rejects the Stoic notion that the earthly realm might be annihilated one day (e.g., *Aet.* 75–76). Hebrews implies that it will be (12:27).
- Philo relies primarily on the Pentateuch for his arguments and uses the Old Testament allegorically more than literally. Hebrews relies as much on the Psalms and other Scriptures outside the law. Hebrews uses the Old Testament more "typologically" than "allegorically."
- Perhaps the most distinctive teaching of Philo was the "allegory of the soul." Philo repeatedly allegorizes Scripture to portray the tension in the soul between the mind, sense perception, and the passions. Hebrews displays no clear knowledge of this allegory. In the end, Hebrews shows greater affinities with the traditions that Philo himself inherited at Alexandria than with Philo's own developments of those traditions.

Figure 3

Hebrews and the Book of Wisdom

Hebrews and Wisdom share enough parallels to suggest that Hebrews's author was aware of this book and certainly that the two come from a common Hellenistic Jewish milieu. The most striking parallel is between Heb. 1:3 and Wis. 7:26:

Wisdom	Hebrews
"she [wisdom] is a *reflection* of eternal light, . . . an image of his [God's] goodness" (Wis. 7:26).	"he [Christ] is a *reflection* of [God's] glory, an impression of his substance" (Heb. 1:3).

In the entirety of the Greek Old Testament and New Testament, the word for "reflection" occurs only in these two places, probably indicating that Hebrews is dependent on the book of Wisdom.

Some other interesting parallels include:

- In keeping with the implicit comparison of Christ to wisdom above, Heb. 1:2 says that Christ is the one "through whom" God made the worlds, much as Wis. 9:1–2 states that God created everything through his word/wisdom.
- Hebrews's statement in 2:14 that the devil holds power over death and Wis. 2:24's statement that death entered the world through the devil's envy.
- Hebrews remarks on the judging aspect of God's "Word," involving a sword (4:12) and Wis. 18:15–16's comparison of the death angel in Egypt to God's judging "Word" carrying a sword.
- The "disciplining" of God's sons through suffering in Heb. 5:8 and 12:4–13, and Wis. 3:5's comparison of the suffering of the righteous *son* of God to God's discipline.
- Hebrews's imagery of Christ sitting at God's right hand (e.g., 1:3, 14; 8:1) and Wis. 9:4's image of wisdom sitting next to God's throne.
- Both have a noticeable body/spirit dualism corresponding to an earth/heaven dualism (e.g., Heb. 9:14; 10:22; 12:18–24; Wis. 9:15).
- Both compare an earthly sanctuary with a heavenly prototype (Heb. 8:5; Wis. 9:8).
- Both recount figures from Israelite history to highlight a particular virtue. In Heb. 11, it is faith; in Wis. 10–19, it is wisdom (although the focus is on wisdom as something from God rather than something possessed by these individuals).
- Both may hold to creation as the ordering of formless matter (Heb. 11:3; Wis. 11:17).

Figure 4

and is permanently thrown out of heaven. According to *Life*, this is the reason the devil had it in for our first parents.[12]

The promised consequence of Adam's sin is death, understood in the original story of Genesis as physical death. However, in the book of Wisdom the devil brings about a spiritual death. Wisdom blends Plato's notion of the soul's immortality with some Jewish themes concerning the punishment of the dead in the afterlife. The result is that the souls of righteous individuals—the sons of God—do not die (2:13, 16–17; 3:1–8). Only the souls of the wicked go on to suffer torment (3:10–11).

The thought of Hebrews closely parallels these traditions in Wisdom, although it also differs in some respects. For example, Hebrews teaches that it is only through Christ that one can truly become a "son of God" from the seed of Abraham (2:16). Not only do the notoriously wicked find themselves trapped by death, but all humanity does. Christ is the first whose prayer to be saved "out of death" is heard because of his "godly fear" (5:7), his life without sin (4:15).[13] In Hebrews, the devil seems to have power over all the spirits of the dead, and probably also over the human body because of its susceptibility to sin. This power of sin presumably comes from the fact that our bodies are a part of the created realm where the devil rules.

The book of Wisdom thus points us toward the Garden of Eden as we probe what Hebrews means when it refers to the devil's power over death. Yet Paul gives us an even better reason. When 1 Cor. 15 speaks of God putting all things under Christ's feet (an allusion to Ps. 8), Paul is speaking of Christ as the "last Adam," the one who undoes the consequences of Adam's transgression. In other words, the history of the use of Ps. 8 in early Christian tradition associated it with Adam's sin in the Garden of Eden.

> A corruptible body burdens the soul, and this earthly tent weighs down the mind with its many cares.
>
> —Wis. 9:15

While individual humans experience death because of their own transgressions (Rom. 5:12), it is the power of sin over the created realm that leads them to transgress in the first place. According to Paul, this power came into the world because of Adam's sin (v. 12). Similarly, death rules in the earthly realm as a consequence of this sin (v. 17). Hebrews would indicate that the devil stands behind this power, an association between sin and evil forces that Paul's writings also make occasionally.[14]

Therefore, while we cannot say for certain, we can make some guesses about how the devil has come to enslave humanity. Enough connections exist to warrant filling in the gaps of Hebrews's argument with elements of Paul's thought and other Jewish traditions. God makes the world with the intention that humanity will stand in a place of glory and honor within it. The devil envies this esteemed position and plots until Adam has sinned, placing human flesh and the created realm under his power. He exercises this power during our human lives through the power of sin over flesh and blood. He wields it most definitively at death, enslaving our human spirits. Under this power, we each sin and fall short of the glory God intended for us, a glory Christ finally makes possible for us to attain.

CHRIST'S SOLUTION: DEFEAT
THE DEVIL'S POWER OVER HUMANITY

We have already caught some glimpses of what an effective solution to humanity's problem might be. If the main obstacle to humanity's glory is the devil's power over death, then Christ must somehow defeat the devil and overcome his power. Since sin confers this power on the devil, we would expect Christ to eliminate sin in some way. Since the devil's power is located in the created realm, it makes sense that Christ's saving work would impact it as well. The most straight forward resolution to the plot would be for God to restore the creation so humanity could finally rule over it.[15]

In actuality, Hebrews presents the resolution of the plot in two stages: (1) Christ defeats the devil's power over death by offering himself as an atoning sacrifice, and (2) God *removes* the created realm and everything in the universe that is "shakable." Christ lives a sinless life and becomes an unblemished sacrifice, atoning for the sins of the "sons of Abraham."[16] Then at the end of the story, God will "shake" the creation and judge it by way of his consuming fire (Heb. 12:27–29). Only that which is "unshakable" will remain.

Christ's Death as a Sacrifice

Because of Adam's sin, the devil controls at least the spirits of the dead and probably the created realm as well. The human weakness for sin helps confer this power on him. We can wonder whether the spirit of a person without sin would be free from such powers. Unfortunately, Hebrews offers little hope for anyone to accomplish such a feat.[17]

Therefore, the first step toward the plot's resolution was for Christ to become a part of the creation, for him to take on flesh and blood and live successfully without sin. Hebrews 2 traces this process. Christ assumed human flesh and blood (2:14); he took on a body (10:5, 10). In keeping with Ps. 8, he became lower than the angels for a little while (2:7). He was made just like those he came to save so he could truly fulfill the psalm on their behalf and become an effective atonement for sin (v. 17). Both the one that sanctifies and those who are being sanctified are of the same sort (v. 11). Humans are Christ's "brothers" (v. 11), and they should put their trust in God for deliverance from the power of death, just as Christ did (2:13; 5:7).

Since the focal point of human enslavement is death, it was fitting for God to "perfect" Jesus through death (2:10). Christ walked through the human experience with all the testings other humans have, yet he did not sin (4:15). For this reason, God heard his prayer to be saved out of death (5:7), and he became a cause of eternal salvation to all who obey him (5:9). God crowned him with the glory and honor intended for all humanity (v. 9). Now he only waits for God to place his enemies under his feet (10:13) so that he can return to earth a second time (9:27).

Unfortunately, even after we have said all these things we are still left somewhat uncertain about how it really works. We have no real specifics about how human sin hands control over to the devil or how sufferings "perfect" Jesus as a cause of salvation. We are unclear whether Christ's sinlessness had always kept him free from the devil's power or whether God still had to take action to save him out of death.[18] These are questions whose answers in part lie deep in the unconscious of the ancient psyche, fundamental assumptions about sacrifices and the spiritual forces that control the world.

Whatever these deeper dynamics were, Hebrews finds the basic answers to these questions in the category of sacrifice. Jesus atoned for the sins of the people (2:17), offering himself blameless to God (9:14). Those who "partake" of him (3:14) and of holy spirit (6:4) are "set apart as holy." They belong to God and the domain of the sacred (10:14); the stain of their sin is cleansed (v. 2). Such language operates on assumptions quite foreign to our modern categories even though we can get the general sense.

The author of Hebrews assumes that "without blood shedding, forgiveness is not possible" (9:22). At first glance, this comment seems to differ significantly from the thought of philosophically inclined Jewish thinkers like Philo. For Philo, far more important than the sacrifices offered in the Jerusalem temple was the attitude of a person making such a sacrifice (*Mos.* 2.24, 107–8). Philo did not think a physical sacrifice was necessary in any way for atonement to take place. Many other Jews shared this opinion, apparently including some of those who preserved the Dead Sea Scrolls (e.g., 1QS 7:3).

Yet the author of Hebrews may actually agree with Philo more than appears at first glance. It seems likely that the author is not really interested in blood or the details of sacrifice in a literal sense.[19] The Levitical cultus is an important part of the story because of the way in which its operation *foreshadows* the true atonement provided through Christ's death. The author highlights blood as an essential element in atonement in order to show the significance of Christ's death—and thus to do away with its necessity forever. Indeed, it is not really physical blood that Christ offers to God in the end, but eternal spirit (Heb. 9:14). Just like Philo and so many other Jews of the time, the author of Hebrews can think of sacrifice metaphorically. For example, he thinks that praise is a kind of sacrifice to God (13:15).

Sacrifices cleansed sin. According to Hebrews, Christ's sacrifice definitively accomplishes such a cleansing because it is a heavenly sacrifice offered in the true, heavenly sanctuary (8:2, 4; 9:11–14, 24; 10:14). The earthly sacrifices did not take away sin (10:2). They were sacrifices of flesh and blood that might cleanse flesh, but they could not cleanse one's "conscience" of sin

(9:9–10).[20] After all, "it is impossible for the blood of bulls and goats to take away sin" (10:4).

At this point the author's argument approaches a contradiction. Hebrews both affirms that physical blood is essential for atonement and yet holds equally that Christ's work was of a spiritual nature in the heavens—not the created realm. This tension in the author's imagery has led to a number of awkward interpretations. For example, some have argued that Christ's sacrifice refers only to his physical death on the cross, while others claim it consists only of his entrance into the heavenly tabernacle.[21] Such interpretations illustrate the problems that arise when one does not recognize the highly metaphorical nature of the author's language.

The literal event that signifies atonement is Christ's death on the cross, and early Christian tradition conceived of it metaphorically as an atoning sacrifice (e.g., Rom. 3:25; 1 Cor. 5:7). Yet Hebrews's argument is unique in that it also metaphorically considers Christ to be a high priest in a *heavenly* sanctuary. His atonement actually works in part for this reason—his "priesthood" is in heaven. In this sense, the metaphor requires the offering to be made in heaven. These two metaphors with their separate origins stand in partial tension with each other.

For the author of Hebrews, the way to appropriate Christ's cleansing is similar to what the book of Acts depicts: (1) repentance, (2) water baptism, and (3) baptism/reception of the Holy Spirit (cf. Acts 2:38). The list of basic Christian teaching in Heb. 6:1–2 mentions repentance, baptisms (plural), and the laying on of hands. The mention of more than one baptism probably corresponds to the two baptisms mentioned also in Acts: water and Spirit baptism. The ritual of laying hands on a person signified receiving the Spirit (cf. Acts 8:18).[22] In keeping with Hebrews's dualism of heavenly/earthly, water baptism relates to the cleansing of one's body while Spirit baptism cleanses the heart/conscience/spirit (Heb. 10:22).

Partaking of "holy spirit" is thus the active element of the salvation process (6:4). Such spirit is heavenly material in our earthly bodies, a "heavenly gift" (6:4). In one sense, it is the "substance of things hoped for" (11:1), a "foretaste of glory divine," a tasting of the "powers of the coming age" (6:5). By partaking of the Christ in this way (3:14) one's sin is atoned for, one has been "perfected," one's sin cleansed (10:1–2).[23]

Again, the exact dynamics of what it means for one's sins to be cleansed or how partaking of spirit defeats the power of death are not discussed. The nature of such events lies in the assumptions of the author relating to human psychology and the world's cosmology, not to mention the categories of purity and defilement. Many of these assumptions are quite foreign to our way of thinking.

However, we can suspect that God's Spirit within us both overcomes the demonic spiritual powers that control the earthly realm (the devil for Hebrews) and also enables us to participate in the heavenly realm. With our spirits cleansed and perfected, they can now ascend to the heavens wherein our new identity lies (12:23).[24] Our spirit has bold and unhindered access to God's presence (e.g., 4:16; 10:19–22). Christ has defeated the devil's power over the sons of Abraham, who no longer need live enslaved by the fear of death throughout the course of their lives (2:15).

The Removal of the Created Realm

Given the way the plot of salvation history begins, a structuralist might hazard a guess about its ending. If the story began when the devil kept humanity from ruling the creation, a structuralist would expect for it to end with humanity in this appointed role. Humanity should finally get the glory and honor God intended us to have in the created realm.

For example, in Paul's version of the story, the creation is "eagerly" waiting for its liberation in the same way humanity is. As Paul says in Rom. 8:19 and 21, "the deep longing of the creation looks expectantly for the revelation of the sons of God. . . . For the creation will also be liberated from the slavery of corruption to have the freedom of the *glory* of the children of God." Paul completes the story's plot in a quite appropriate way. Since the problem of the story is the fact that humanity is unable to experience glory and honor in the creation, God liberates and *transforms* the creation. God makes it possible for the creation to participate in the glorification of God's children.

A structuralist might diagram Paul's solution to the plot in this way:

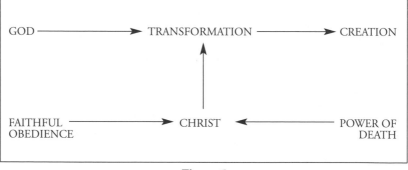

Figure 5

God transforms the creation in a way that frees it from the power of sin, and he does this through Christ's faithful obedience to the point of death (Phil. 2:8; Rom. 3:25; Gal. 2:20).

For Paul, part of the creation's transformation is the metamorphosis of our physical bodies into spiritual bodies. While Adam's transgression brought the experience and power of death into the created realm (Rom. 5:12), Christ's righteous act brings the hope of resurrection and eternal life (Rom. 6:17, 21; 1 Cor. 15:21–22). It is important for Paul to think of this future resurrection as an *embodied* existence. He assumes that embodiment is an essential component of resurrection, even if it is a spiritual embodiment (e.g., 1 Cor. 15:35).

So while the "first" Adam became a living *soul*, presumably including flesh, the "last" Adam became a life-giving *spirit* (1 Cor. 15:45).[25] Christ has made possible a resurrected body constituted by heavenly, spiritual material (vv. 47–49). On the other hand, a body made up of the material of this current, corrupted creation is incompatible with the coming kingdom: "flesh and blood cannot inherit the kingdom of God" (v. 50). Although Christ is the firstfruits of this resurrection and has already set it in motion, the final resurrection of those in Christ will take place in the future along with the transformation of the rest of the creation.

While the author of Hebrews probably inherited these interpretations of Ps. 8 from the Pauline tradition, he seems to depart at several points from the way Paul resolves the plot. While Paul is sympathetic to the creation's plight, the author of Hebrews associates the created realm with the old age that is passing away. Hebrews is interested in the *removal* of the created realm rather than its liberation (e.g., Heb. 1:10–12; 12:25–29). The fundamental orientation of Hebrews is away from any association with the earthly and is redirected toward the heavenly as our true homeland (e.g., 11:13–16; 12:18–24; 13:14). This shift in the plot probably reflects some of the author's philosophical presuppositions—and possibly a shift in the political situation since the days of Paul.

A structuralist might diagram Hebrews's solution to the plot in the following way:

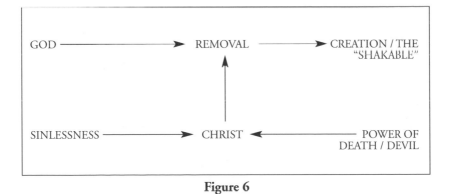

Figure 6

While Hebrews echoes the traditional Christian notion of the resurrection of bodies (e.g., 6:2; cf. 11:35), its author shows no real commitment to a continuity between our physical bodies and our future spiritual existence. Hebrews seems to view the spirit as something detachable from our body in such a way that it can reach heaven even while a person is still on earth (e.g., 12:23). And while Christ's blood is essential to the process of salvation, it is "through eternal spirit" that he offers himself blameless to God (9:14). Even the allusion to Christ's resurrection in Heb. 13:20 uses a word that pictures Christ's spirit coming up spatially from the realm of the dead rather than the more usual word for resurrection that had overtones of re-embodiment.[26]

One might almost say that human salvation is the removal of one's spirit from the power and influence of the created realm and the devil that seems to control that realm. God accomplishes this goal by removing everything that is "shakable" from the universe.[27] In a sense, God changes the course of the plot. While he intended for humanity to rule the creation with glory and honor, he instead places humanity in a position of glory and honor in heaven. The plot is successful because we receive what we were supposed to receive, even though we do not receive it in the way God originally intended.

We can also learn about the ending of the plot by looking at why it has not finished yet. In the period between Christ's sacrifice and the judgment, Christ is waiting for God to subdue his enemies. Hebrews 10:13, as 1 Cor. 15:25–27, indicates that while Christ has largely fulfilled Ps. 8, he does not yet have all things under his feet.

Paul and Hebrews associated Ps. 8:4–6 with Ps. 110:1, both of which speak of the submission of something under feet. It is not difficult to see why the early Christians would have connected these two verses:

> "You subjected all things under his *feet*."
> Ps. 8:7 (LXX)

> "Sit on my right hand until I place your enemies as a footstool for your *feet*."
>
> Ps. 110:1

One common method of Jewish interpretation connected two texts if they used similar words. We call this "catchword" technique *gezerah shewa*. Paul and Hebrews associated these two specific verses because both entail the subjection of something beneath someone's feet. Taking them together, they concluded that the last step in salvation required Christ's enemies to be placed under his feet. When this happens, he will return to earth (Heb. 9:27).

Hebrews does not explicitly tell us who these enemies are, but the apostle Paul once again may fill in some of the gaps in our knowledge. For Paul, these enemies are primarily spiritual forces: "rulers," "authorities," and "powers" (1 Cor. 15:24). They are the rulers of this earthly realm and this current age (2:8). These are some of the "elemental spirits" that control the creation (Gal. 4:3). The last such power that God will put under Christ's feet is death (1 Cor. 15:26). As the devil is in Hebrews, Paul intrinsically connects these powers to the current state of the created

gezerah shewa A Jewish interpretive method that interprets one scriptural text by linking it with another text that uses similar words.

realm. Human glory is tied up with their defeat, especially the defeat of the devil.[28]

CONCLUSION

Psalm 8 captured the story of salvation history in a nutshell for the author of Hebrews. God created humanity with the intention that we would rule over the creation and that we would have a place of honor within this earthly realm, but apparently the devil was jealous that God would give such glory to a creature made lower than him. He conspired against the first human, Adam, and led him to sin. In consequence, the devil gained power over death and the created realm as well.

God's solution was a blameless sacrifice that atoned for the "sons of Abraham." Hebrews applies this title to any human who might partake of Christ. God prepared a body for Jesus, like the flesh and blood of humanity, so that he might destroy the devil and his power over the creation. Christ underwent the human experience; he was tested as all humans are tested, yet he did not sin. As he approached death, he prayed to the one who could save him out of that realm. God heard his prayer and brought his spirit up from the realm of the dead, creating a way to the heavenly realm that was not previously open (cf. Heb. 10:20).

The ultimate resolution to the plot will come when God removes all that is "shakable" in the universe, the created realm in particular. The consuming fire of God will finally destroy death and the devil. The spirits of the perfected righteous will eternally enjoy an unshakable kingdom in a heavenly city.

Chapter 3

The Celebration of the Enthroned Son

THE CHALLENGE OF HEBREWS 1:5–14

Many have puzzled over how Heb. 1 connects to the remainder of the epistle.[1] At first glance, its chain—or *catena*—of citations from the Old Testament (1:5–14) seems somewhat unrelated to the motifs that follow in the later chapters, not least that of Christ as high priest. Indeed, some commentators interpret Hebrews almost as if it were a set of unrelated contrasts between Christ and various other important figures.[2] In the manner of their presentation, the contrast between Christ and the angels shows that Christ is truly great, but it does not clearly relate to the other contrasts of the epistle.

This apparent disconnection has led some interpreters to suppose that the catena existed in some form independently of Hebrews and that the author inserted it into his sermon with a few modifications.[3] Harold Attridge even suggests that some of the tensions in the Christology of the epistle have resulted from this incorporation of material.[4] Certainly some of these verses did come from early Christian tradition (e.g., Ps. 2 and 110), and we do know of collections of quotations from this period.[5] The suggestion that Hebrews might have incorporated such a collection is thus plausible.

However, it was a scholar by the name of G. B. Caird who probably gave us the key to interpreting this chapter in relation to the rest of the epistle. In a brief article titled "The Exegetical Method of the Epistle to the Hebrews," he made the largely undeveloped suggestion that Heb. 1 is best understood in the light of Ps. 8, as cited in Heb. 2.[6] Hebrews's use of this psalm implies that while Christ became lower than the angels in order to atone for sins, he is now crowned with glory and honor. He has now attained a status greater than theirs. In this light, the contrast of Heb. 1 centers on Christ's current state of exaltation, since he has accomplished his mission on earth.

When we read it in this way, the catena of Heb. 1 presents the opening scene of Act II in the story of salvation history.[7] Christ has already entered into the heavenly Holy of Holies and atoned for the sins of God's people. Heaven is celebrating the accomplishment of Christ's earthly mission as he is enthroned as royal Son. In terms of Hebrews's rhetoric, the author begins at the high point of the story in order to grab the attention of his audience and put them in the proper mood for what follows. The relevance of the contrast will become apparent enough as the author develops his argument.

Caird's interpretation fits Heb. 1 with Heb. 2 beautifully—so beautifully, in fact, that one might wonder why this view is not the consensus of scholarship. The answer comes as soon as one turns to the actual citations of 1:5–14. Verse 6 speaks of Christ being greater than the angels when God leads him "into the habitable world." This statement sounds a lot like the appearance of angels to shepherds in Luke 2. Verses 10–12 speak of Christ as the one who "founded the earth," seeming to assign Christ a role in creation. In other words, the timing of the actual verses in Heb. 1 at least *sounds* far more diverse than Caird's suggestion, which places the focus of all these verses on the exalted Christ—long after the creation of the world or Christ's arrival on earth.[8] For several reasons, the chain of quotations seems much more like a general contrast of Christ with the angels *at all points of his existence*, not just when he was exalted to heaven.

Nevertheless, we have good reason to think that Caird's suggestion is basically correct and that our "common sense" is misleading us in this case. When we approach the text with the presuppositions of its first audience, the chapter is indeed focused on the exalted Christ at the point of his "enthronement." Christ becomes lower than the angels in order to accomplish salvation. Therefore, his return to an exalted state signals salvation's accomplishment. A contrast of Christ with the angels is thus a fitting introduction to a sermon about the effectiveness of Christ's atoning death.

Further, the author associates angels with the mediation and administration of the old covenant. They are ministering spirits sent on behalf of God's people in the earthly realm (Heb. 1:14). Angels will not be in such a position of leadership in the coming, heavenly world (2:5). By showing the superiority of Christ to the angels, the author implies that the new covenant inaugurated by Christ is also greater than the Jewish law, which was commanded through angels.

Finally, the immediate context of the catena and the tradition history behind some of the individual quotations (that is, the way those verses were used by Christians before Hebrews was written) indicate that the focus of the chain *is* on the exalted Christ. The verses paint a picture of Christ's enthronement as royal Son, destined to rule over all things, with the angels as servants bowing in obeisance to their king. When we read 1:5–14 in this way, Heb. 1 fits in beautifully with the rest of the author's argument in the epistle.

> **tradition history**   The way a particular term, concept, or Scripture was used and developed in the history of a tradition, such as early Christianity.

HEBREWS 1 IN THE LIGHT OF PSALM 8

In the previous chapter, we discussed the way in which the author of Hebrews interprets Ps. 8 and uses it in his argument. Drawing on earlier Christian traditions that regarded Christ as the "Last Adam," the author reads the text on two levels. First, he reads the psalm as a statement of God's ideal for humanity, an ideal unattained because of Adam's sin. Second, he reads it as a description of the process to which God subjected Christ in order to make that ideal finally possible for his people. Like the "seed of Abraham" (Heb. 2:16), Jesus became lower than the angels (i.e., became human, fleshly, earthly) for a little while. He suffered death as humanity does, yet without having sin. He thus defeated the devil, the one holding the power of death. God found it fitting to "perfect" Christ through death so that he might "lead many sons to glory" (v. 10) in fulfillment of the psalm.

In this light, it seems fitting for Hebrews to begin with a celebration of the exalted Christ. The first chapter of this sermon reads like a ticker-tape parade at the end of a war in which Christ has been victorious. It parades Christ before its audience as victor in the battle against sin, death, and the devil by announcing his exaltation to a position higher than the angels. The "little while" of Ps. 8 is over, and salvation is accomplished.

The author tells us in Heb. 8:1 that the main point of his rhetoric is that Christ is a heavenly high priest. This "high priesthood" is a metaphorical way for the author to say that Christ's death provides the only effective atonement for sins.[9] Therefore, Christ's entrance into the heavenly Holy of Holies is the same event as his exaltation/enthronement at the right hand of God. As such, it signifies the accomplishment of a definitive atonement. If this accomplishment is the main point of the epistle's rhetoric, then the author's introductory contrast between Christ and the angels is extremely relevant to his later argument— Christ's exaltation implies the availability of true salvation.

Since the author understood Ps. 8 both in terms of humanity and Christ, he saw in its words the lordship of Christ over God's creation. As God had originally intended for humanity, he puts all things under Christ's feet. Unlike the current world, the world to come will not be subject to angels (2:5). Rather, Christ and those he leads to glory will rule. When we speak of lordship and subjection, we have entered the territory of kingship and rulers. It is thus no surprise that the catena uses royal, "messianic" language from the Jewish Scriptures in order to describe the exalted Christ. Its chain of citations reads like a liturgy for the enthronement of a Davidic king.

ANGELS AND THE OLD COVENANT

In at least one sense, the catena of Heb. 1 does stand apart from the material that immediately follows: It is almost in a different genre. The difference reminds us somewhat of those places in the New Testament where an author turns suddenly from argument to "hymnic" language in reference to Christ.[10] This shift in tone and fervor is no doubt part of the reason some have seen this string of quotes as an insertion of previously existing material into the text of Hebrews.

The catena is worshipful and lofty, including words of praise to Christ. The argument that follows is more "logical" in the sense of ancient rhetoric—it aims to persuade *by reasoning*.[11] The catena presents an argument as well, but it is more poetic and no doubt appealed strongly to the *emotions* of the audience. It is stirring and focused. It bombards the audience's senses with the triumphant greatness of Christ without immediately pointing out its relevance to the arguments that follow. It is like an invocation that stands in its own right, yet that we only recognize as relevant to the sermon later on in the service. It begins the story *in medias res* in order to catch our attention and leave us desperate to find out what has gone before and what will follow.

Hebrews 2:1–4 thus bring a "change of gears" as teaching turns to preaching. These verses still mention angels and Christ, but the focus is no longer their relationship to one another. Rather, it is on the relationship between the two covenants they have each mediated. Some would argue that the author has moved on to a new point, as if he had completely finished the thought of the previous chapter. The approaches of Heb. 1 and 2:1–4 are different enough that some interpreters see any connection as weak and superficial.[12] They do not believe that the author himself made a correlation between Heb. 1 and his later argument concerning the two covenants.

However, if the catena of Heb. 1 is a "hymnic" celebration of Christ's enthronement, then the distance is more one of genre and purpose than thought or category. Although it may stand somewhat on its own, Heb. 1 is nonetheless fully relevant to the remainder of the author's argument. It is appropriate because it implies the main point of the epistle: the salvation Christ has accomplished. Moreover, it is very relevant to the author's contrast between the two covenants, even if this contrast is not made very explicit in Heb. 1.

We know that many first-century Jews believed that angels had mediated the law to Moses, but the extent of angelic involvement in the earthly realm went far beyond this particular act. Angels were ministering spirits to God's people, intermediaries who were sent by God to accomplish his purposes.[13] They also seem to have guarded the holiness expressed in the law. Therefore, the contrast of Christ with the angels had significant implications for the way in which God was now relating to the world. The audience of Hebrews would have appreciated these further dimensions of the contrast far more than we do from our current vantage point.

On the most basic level, the New Testament unanimously affirms that angels mediated the law. Stephen's speech in Acts 7 argues that the members of the Sanhedrin reverenced the law as something *"commanded by angels,"* although they failed to keep it. Paul states similarly in Gal. 3:19 that the law was *"commanded through angels* in the hand of a mediator." Hebrews 2:2 thus says nothing unusual when it refers to the law as the "word spoken *through angels*."

These comments allude to a common belief among Jews of that day: God gave the law to Moses by way of angelic mediation. Josephus, a Jewish historian of the late first century C.E., indicates that the Jews learned God's laws "through angels sent by God" (*Ant.* 15.136). The book of *Jubilees*, written over two hundred years before Hebrews, similarly records that the Lord commanded the "angel of the presence" to write down the law for Moses (*Jub.* 1:27, 29; 2:1).[14] Therefore, a contrast between angels and Christ would be a suitable preface to a contrast between the Mosaic law and the new covenant.

Yet Hebrews itself indicates that the connection between angels and the old order is more extensive than this one act. The climax of the catena indicates that angels are "ministering spirits sent to serve those about to inherit salvation" (Heb. 1:14). When the author picks up this train of thought again in 2:5, he notes that angels will not rule the coming world.[15] The implication is both that this current world *is* subjected in some way to the rule of angels and that this role in relation to humanity is about to end. The coming of Christ signals a transition in rule and authority from the angels to Christ (and humanity).

We conclude that the principal role of angels in salvation history relates to God's people prior to salvation—that is, in the earthly realm in Act I of the plot. Of course, they will also praise God in heaven for eternity (cf. 12:22), but the contrast of Heb. 1 focuses on the role they have played in relation to the earthly realm. Hebrews 1:6 indicates that God uses angels as winds and flames to do his bidding, elements of the earthly realm (cf. 4 Ezra 8:22). Perhaps they were even at Mt. Sinai in such forms: burning fire, darkness, gloom, and storm (Heb. 12:18; cf. Deut. 4:11). The Greek translation of Deut. 33:2 places angels at Mt. Sinai, and Jub. 2:2 indicates that they can take forms such as those pictured in Heb. 12:18.[16]

> On the first day he [God] created the heavens, which are above, and the earth, and the waters and all the spirits which minister before him: the angels of the presence, and the angels of sanctification, and the angels of the *spirit of fire*, and the angels of the *spirit of the winds*, and the angels of the *spirit of the clouds and darkness* and snow and hail and frost. . . .
> —Jub. 2:2

Other passages from the literature of the period seem to indicate that angels served as guardians of holiness in connection with the law. The Rule of the Congregation from Qumran notes that it is inappropriate for anyone who is lame, blind, or who has any visible blemish to be a part of the assembly because "the angels of holiness are among their congregation."[17] Such a standard of holiness appears in Lev. 21:17–23. There, no priest with a similar bodily defect can come near God's tabernacle. One interpretation of 1 Cor. 11:10 also sees the angels as the guardians of proper order in worship.[18] A woman must not pray or prophesy with her head uncovered "because of the angels."

Whatever the "worship of angels" might be in Col. 2:18, this verse strongly associates it with a strict observance of the law (cf. Col. 2:14): "Do not grasp. Do not taste. Do not touch" (v. 21). Colossians here, as Gal. 4:3 does in a slightly different way, connects law observance with the "basic principles" of the earthly realm, elements under the control of the spiritual "powers and authorities" of the earth. While the situation of these two passages is not exactly the same as that of Hebrews, enough similarities exist to support the case for an association between angels, the law, and the earthly realm.

Therefore, the author and audience of Hebrews would have seen the relevance of Heb. 1 to the later contrast between the two covenants. When the author argues that Christ has made the law obsolete, he also implies that the role of the angels as its guardians and administrators has come to an end. Further, Christ's enthronement as king of the coming world implies that he has superceded their role as the rulers of this age. A contrast between the enthroned Christ and the servant angels once more proves to be an appropriate opening to the epistle.

We should mention one further possibility before we move on to the actual text of the catena. Scholars have long suggested that some situation stands behind the contrast of Heb. 1. Perhaps the audience viewed Christ as an angel or perhaps they worshiped angels.[19] By contrasting Christ with the angels, the author would put both into their appropriate categories. As we have shown, neither of these hypotheses is really necessary to explain the catena's existence, although we cannot completely rule them out either.

Another possibility is that the audience of Hebrews believed angels to atone for their sins in a heavenly tabernacle. The Qumran document *Songs of the Sabbath Sacrifice* speaks of angels as "priests who serve in the presence of the holy king" (1:8) and who intercede for those who have turned from sin (v. 16). The Testament of Levi similarly notes that the archangels of the highest heaven offer atoning sacrifices for the sins of ignorance committed by the righteous (3:5). If the audience of Hebrews knew such traditions, the epistle's argument as a whole would be quite appropriate.

The evidence is of course insufficient to prove or disprove any of these hypotheses completely. It is enough to show that there are any number of more specific ways that the catena of Heb. 1 might have related to the contrast that followed. At the very least, the strong connection between angels, the law, the earthly realm, and the old covenant makes the catena a fitting preface to the subsequent argument. Caird's hypothesis is once again vindicated. Becoming "lower" than the angels involves a submission to their rule under the old covenant, while the crowning of Christ with glory and honor implies a shift of authority to Christ and the new covenant he mediates.

HEBREWS 1:5–14 AS CHRIST'S ENTHRONEMENT

Probably the strongest objections against this interpretation of Heb. 1 come from those who believe the catena contrasts Christ and the angels at all points of his existence. Many scholars believe that 1:5–14 cover the whole spectrum from Christ's preexistence to his earthly life and later exaltation.[20] Our common sense—particularly as the creeds of the church have influenced it—tends to move us away from the original nuances of the text.

On the other hand, both the literary and traditional contexts of these verses point us to Christ's exaltation for its timing. The verses that immediately precede the string of citations state:

> After he made a cleansing for sins, he sat on the right hand of Majesty in the heavenlies, *having become* as much greater than the angels as the superior greatness of the name he has inherited. (1:3b–4)

The word translated here as "having become" most naturally refers to a transition from an old status to a new one, that is, from a status lower than the angels to a "name" greater than theirs.[21] Such an exaltation is no surprise in the light of the use of Ps. 8 in the following chapter, which notes that Christ became lower than the angels "for a little while." Therefore, the verse preceding the catena clearly relates it to Christ's exaltation above the angels *after* his atoning death.

> 5. For to which of the angels has he [God] said at any time,
> *"You are my Son; today I have given you birth,"* and again,
> *"I will be a Father to him, and he himself will be a Son to me"*?
> 6. And again, when he leads the Firstborn into the habitable world, he says,
> *"And let all the angels of God worship him."*

Hebrews 1:5

We can imagine several possible reactions to Heb. 1:5. One might be puzzlement at the suggestion that there was a "today" when God "gave birth" to Christ. Another person might think of Jesus' earthly birth when reading this verse. After all, it mentions a birth, and the angels seem to worship Jesus in verse 6 just as the shepherds did in Luke 2:8–14.

Some readers of a more orthodox bent might hear overtones of the Nicene Creed in the verse. The creed states that Christ was "eternally begotten of the Father . . . begotten, not made, of one Being with the Father. . . ." Another reader might even remember that God addressed Jesus as Son after his baptism (Matt. 3:17; Mark 1:11; Luke 3:22; John 1:34). Perhaps God "adopted" Jesus as his Son after his baptism.

In the final analysis, however, it seems fairly clear that this verse relates to the resurrected and exalted Christ. We have already mentioned the immediate context of Heb. 1:3–4: Christ's session at the right hand of God as the attainment of a "name" that is greater than that of the angels. When the author begins the following verse with the word "for," he creates the expectation that what he is going to say will back up the claim of the preceding verse. Hebrews 1:5 does exactly this when it notes that God never bestowed the title of "Son" on an angel. "Son" is thus the name Christ inherits at the point of his exaltation, a name as much greater than the name of "angel" as the exalted status of Christ is greater than angelic status.

It is not natural for us to think of sonship as an office or position, although the idea of an adopted son comes close. Yet the original meaning of Ps. 2:7 and 2 Sam. 7:14—the two verses cited in Heb. 1:5—relate to the office of a king. The same can be said of the way in which later Judaism understood their meaning.

The phrase "son(s) of God" is used in several ways in the Jewish Scriptures. Ironically, it *can* be used of angelic beings or of the gods of the nations (e.g., Job 1:6; Ps. 82:6). God refers to Israel as his son as well (Hos. 11:1), and the Wisdom of Solomon considers a righteous person to be a "son of God" (e.g., Wis. 2:18). More important, Hebrews and the New Testament in general call Christ "Son of God" on the basis of royal traditions that used this language of a Davidic king—a king from the lineage of David.

Second Samuel 7:14 provides a good illustration of this use of "son of God": "I will be a Father to him, and he himself will be a Son to me." The context is a message from the Lord to David regarding Solomon. God tells David that the relationship between him and Solomon will be like that of father to son. Jews at the time of Christ understood this verse as a reference to an anointed king—or royal "messiah"—who would come to restore Israel's kingdom.[22] A document from Qumran, Cave 4, *Florilegium*, uses this verse in reference to the "Branch of David" (11) who was coming to "raise up the hut of David which has fallen" (12–13), that is, restore Israel's kingdom. Therefore, Hebrews quite likely refers to Christ as someone in the office of royal messiah when it uses this title in relation to Christ.

It is interesting that 4QFlor also refers to Ps. 2, although not specifically to 2:7—"You are my Son; today I have given you birth." This psalm is a royal psalm that originally referred to a human king. It is often suggested that it was used as part of a coronation or enthronement ceremony.[23] The early Christians seem to have understood it similarly, except as the enthronement of the Messiah as "Son of God."

The use of this verse elsewhere in the New Testament provides us with one of the strongest reasons for reading the catena in terms of Christ's resurrection/ exaltation. The verse probably stands in the background of Rom. 1:3, which states that Christ is one who:

1. came from the seed of David according to the flesh and
2. was *appointed "Son of God" in power* according to the Spirit of holiness, *on the basis of his resurrection from the dead.*

Acts 13:33 is even clearer when it has Peter say,

> God fulfilled this promise to their children, us, *when he raised Jesus*, as also it is written in the second psalm, *"You are my Son; today I have given you birth."*

The tradition history of the verse thus points strongly to the very same meaning the context of Heb. 1:5 does, namely, that Christ's exaltation to the right hand of God is also his enthronement as God's royal Son. Similar references could be cited with regard to the titles "Lord" and "Christ." The earliest material in the New Testament indicates that Jesus received these titles most meaningfully at the point of his resurrection (e.g., Acts 2:36; Rom. 10:9; Phil. 2:11).

Of course, Hebrews and the rest of the New Testament also refer to Jesus as Son before his death (e.g., Heb. 5:8; Mark 1:11), but such references work because Christian tradition came to view the earthly Jesus through the lens of what he was destined to accomplish. In the period before his resurrection, we can think of him as a kind of "heir apparent" to the throne—he can always be called Son because his destiny is certain.[24]

The use of Ps. 8 in Heb. 2 also supports the idea that Heb. 1:5 refers to Christ's enthronement as king. When Christ is crowned with glory and honor, he is no longer in a status lower than the angels—God has put everything under his feet. Hebrews 1:5 thus fits perfectly with the psalm since it combines the coronation of Christ as king with him gaining a higher status than the angels. In short, the evidence is overwhelmingly in favor of taking Heb. 1:5 as a reference to the enthronement of Jesus as royal Son of God at God's right hand in fulfillment of Ps. 8.

Hebrews 1:6

"*And again, whenever he leads his firstborn into the habitable world he says, 'And let all the angels of God worship him.'*" It would be a mistake to isolate this verse from its immediate context. We must read Heb. 1:5 and 6 together, for verse 6 completes a trilogy of opening citations, each of which relates to the enthronement of Christ as royal Son of God. Hebrews 1:5 demonstrates Christ's enthronement in terms of what God says to him and about him. Hebrews 1:6 demonstrates Christ's enthronement by what God says to his subjects. If verse 5 presents us with the enthronement of the king, verse 6 presents us with the servants of the king bowing in obeisance.

A number of critical issues flow out of this verse. For example, the citation does not correspond to any verse in the standard Hebrew text of the Jewish Scriptures, although it comes close to the text of the Song of Moses in the Septuagint (Deut. 32:43, specifically). However, the exact text does occur in a version of the Song of Moses found in the Odes (2:43). A Hebrew fragment of the verse found at Qumran may indicate that this rendition of the verse is actually closer to the original than the standard Masoretic text.[25]

Another issue is whether the verse should be translated "and *again*, when he leads his firstborn in the habitable world" or "and when he leads his firstborn into the habitable world *again*." The latter translation

parousia The arrival of Christ on earth from heaven on the day of judgment.

would point to the second coming of Christ (the *parousia*) as the time when God commands the angels to worship him. The Greek could theoretically be translated in either way.

However, if we look at the structure of verses 5–6, we can see that the author uses the word "again" twice in order to link both 2 Sam. 7:14 and Deut. 32:43 to Ps. 2:7:

> To which of the angels has he said . . ., "You are my Son . . ."
>
> Ps. 2:7

> *and again*, "I will be a Father . . ."
>
> 2 Sam. 7:14

> *and again* he says . . . "Let the angels . . ."
>
> Deut. 32:43

The tendency to isolate Heb. 1:6 from its context has contributed strongly to its misinterpretation. The author is using this quotation to bolster the same claim he has made by the other two citations.

Probably the most controversial aspect of this verse is the meaning of the word I have rendered as "habitable world"—*oikoumene*. This word normally refers to the civilized world, the inhabited world of the earth. For this reason interpreters commonly understand the verse in terms of Christ's incarnation, when God leads Christ into the world.

On the other hand, we can make a strong case that the word refers to the heavenly world. When God exalts Christ to his right hand as king, he leads his firstborn Son into heaven and commands his angels to bow in obeisance. Indeed, it is possible that the author uses this word *precisely because* of the irony it creates. The author will imply at several points in the epistle that God's people are "strangers and foreigners on the earth" (Heb. 11:13). "Here we have no lasting city," Heb. 13:14 proclaims. Our true homeland, the truly "civilized" or "habitable" world is not on earth, but it is in heaven.

Hebrews 2:5 confirms this understanding of the word: "it is not to angels that God has subjected the coming *habitable world* of which we are speaking." This verse sheds much light on Heb. 1:6, for it reveals (1) that the author thinks of the world to come as an *oikoumene,* and (2) that the angels do not rule that world *but rather serve*. Therefore, the broader context of Hebrews supports this interpretation of the verse.

The immediate context does as well. Not only is the citation linked to verses that refer to Christ's enthronement as royal Son, but the verse itself speaks of Christ as God's "firstborn." This term provides us with yet another example of royal language in the Psalms. In Ps. 89:27 God says of David, "I myself will make him the *firstborn*, the highest among the kings of the earth." Given that early Christian tradition applied this title to Christ at the point of his resurrection, we have yet more evidence that the verse refers to the point when God seats Christ at his right hand.

Finally, if we return again to the context provided by Ps. 8, we realize that Heb. 1:6 cannot refer to Christ's entrance into the earthly realm as a human, for it is exactly at this point that Christ became *lower* than the angels. In short, to read this verse in relation to the earthly Jesus requires one to rip the catena out of the epistle, as some do when they view it as an insertion of foreign material. On the other hand, Occam's razor asks that we take the simplest explanation as the most likely. Taking Heb. 1:6 as a reference to Christ's entrance into the heavenly realm is not only the simplest interpretation; it makes the verse fit perfectly with the rest of the epistle.

Hebrews 1:7–12

The basic structure of these verses is very clear in Greek. An "on the one hand" in verse 7 contrasts with an "on the other hand" in verse 8. Thus the entirety of Heb. 1:8–12 contrasts with verse 7. The one citation in regard to the angels contrasts with two citations concerning the Son.

> 7.   On the one hand, he says to the angels . . .
> 8–9.   On the other hand, to the Son [he says],
>   a. "Your throne, O God, . . ."
> and   b. "You, O Lord, . . ."

What the author primarily contrasts is the respective roles and functions that God has assigned to the angels and Christ respectively. These roles are quite simply distinguished: The angels are servants; Christ is king. The angels are winds and flames; Christ is "God" and "Lord." Here is another place where our common sense is bound to lead us away from the correct interpretation. We will have to be careful to read the verses as their original readers would have and not as they appear to us.

Hebrews 1:7

We mentioned this verse earlier in the chapter as an example of how Hebrews associates angels with aspects of the created realm. The author took a psalm that said God makes winds and flames his messengers and made it say that God sometimes makes his messengers (i.e., his angels) into winds and flames.[26] We also quoted *Jub.* 2:2, which speaks of angels as fire, winds, clouds, darkness, snow, hail, and frost. We mentioned that the Septuagint version of Deut. 33:2 indicated that angels were present at the giving of the law, and we hypothesized that the fire, darkness, gloom, and storm in Heb. 12:18 might refer to them. The verse is thus about some of the varying earthly forms angels take in order to accomplish God's purposes on earth.

> 7. And, *on the one hand,* he says to the angels,
>   "the one who makes his angels winds and his servants flames of fire"
>   (cf. Ps. 104:4).

The author himself interprets the citation for us at the conclusion of Hebrews 1 when he poses the rhetorical question, "Are they not all ministering spirits sent to serve those about to inherit salvation?" The word *ministering* here is the same one used in Heb. 1:7 to refer to the angels, and the word *pneuma* here, which means both *spirit* and *wind*, is the same in the two verses as well. Therefore, when the author says God makes his angelic ministers into winds and flames, he is referring to the ways in which God utilizes them to minister to his people on earth. They are God's servants, just like Moses in 3:5. On the other hand, Christ is a Son in God's household.

Hebrews 1:8–9

This passage is quite striking—it is one of very few in the New Testament that refer to Christ as "God" rather than as the "*Son of* God" or some other title. Once again, the citation comes from a royal psalm, Ps. 45, which was written for the wedding of a king. For this reason we must be very careful not to read it in terms of later Christian theology—it originally referred to a human being.[27]

The context gives us several reasons to read this citation as another reference to Christ as enthroned king at God's right hand. On the one hand, the citation itself has all the markings of our argument so far. The one who is initially addressed as "God" in the quote has companions; he has been exalted in their midst. These companions could of course be Christ's brothers in Heb. 2. He shared their flesh and blood and has now been anointed as "Christ" at the point of his exaltation. Or it could refer to the angels of the immediate context. Christ has become higher than they before their very eyes, in their very presence. Both readings fit with a focus on the enthroned Christ.

> 8. But, on the other hand, to the Son [he says],
> "Your throne, O God, is forever and ever,
> And the rod of straightness is the rod of your kingdom.
> 9. "You loved righteousness and hated lawlessness,
> Therefore God, your God, anointed you with the oil of rejoicing
> in the presence of your companions" (cf. Ps. 45:6–7).

The title "God" here is probably yet another way of expressing what the titles "Son" and "firstborn" have already expressed in the previous verses. For example, the one whom this verse addresses initially as "God" is subordinate to yet another "God" who anointed him, as was the case with the king the psalm originally addressed. This king may have been God's representative on earth to the people, but he was still responsible to the supreme God who had anointed him as king in the first place. Unfortunately, we cannot be certain whether the author had any thought of the original context in his use of the verse.[28]

However, the differentiation between the two "Gods" opens the door for seeing Christ's position in this verse as equivalent to the office of "Son of God"—a royal office appointed by God, "the Father." The fact that Christ is "anointed" into this position supports this interpretation. Indeed, the citation evokes the title of "anointed one" or "Christ."

We must then ask how these verses relate specifically to Heb. 1:7, the verse with which verses 8–9 are in contrast. We have already indicated that the main point of contrast is one of role or status. The angels are ministers and servants of God. On the other hand, Christ is a king of higher status than that of his companions.

A second point of contrast becomes clear with the statement that Christ's throne is "forever." Not only are winds and flames associated with the earthly realm, they are also transitory.[29] They are passing; they come and go. Heraclitus, a Greek philosopher prior to Socrates, saw fire as the basic element of the universe, and he accordingly believed that the entire world was in a constant state of change. "You cannot step into the same river twice," he said. Before you have put your foot in a second time, the river has changed. The New Testament itself provides us with a glimpse of wind's nature in John 3:8: "The wind (*pneuma*) blows wherever it wants and you hear its sound, but you do not know where it has come from or where it goes."

In contrast to this transitory picture of the angels is the permanence of Christ. His throne is forever! It will not come and go, nor will it change. We, if not the author, can see a parable in this contrast between the role of angels and the role of Christ. They are ministering spirits sent to serve those about to inherit salvation. Yet this function is about to end. Christ's role, on the other hand, is a permanent office that will last forever.

Hebrews 1:10–12

Superficially, this citation poses the greatest challenge to Caird's basic interpretation of the catena.[30] A common-sense reading of these verses out of context gives us the strong impression that the author is contrasting the angels with Christ as creator—the preexistent Christ rather than the resurrected Christ. Although I suspect that the author is being far more profound, all that is necessary to fit these verses in with the remainder of the chapter is to show that the author's *reason* for using the quotation relates directly to Christ's enthronement. If the *focus* of the author's use of the quote is not on Christ as creator but on some other aspect of the citation relating to his enthronement, then the question of whether Christ is envisaged as the literal creator of the world is moot.

The fact that these verses are used in direct contrast with Heb. 1:7 provides them with exactly such a focus. As the use of Ps. 45 highlighted the *eternal* aspect of Christ's role as Son in contrast to the *transitory* role of the angels in the old covenant, so the focus of Heb. 1:10–12 is on the permanence of Christ in contrast to the earthly realm where the angels minister temporarily. Psalm 102:25–27 indicates that the created realm is destined to perish; it will be changed like a garment.[31] In contrast, Christ the Lord has a place of permanence in the overall story.

We have already shown that the author associates angels not only with the old covenant, but also with the created realm in general. That is not to say that all angels serve in the created realm or that those angels that do will perish along with the creation—but Heb. 1 is primarily concerned with those angels whose current role is to minister to God's people under the old covenant, the guardians of God's holiness as expressed in the law, the current mediators between God and the earth. They serve as winds and flames, elements of the created realm. On the other hand, Christ stands before and after the created realm. His destiny is not linked to the destiny of the earthly realm.

> 10. And
> "You, O Lord, founded the earth at the beginning,
> and the heavens are the works of your hands.
> *They* will perish,
> but *you* remain
> As a covering you will wrap them up;
> as a garment, they also will be changed
> But *you* are the same,
> And your years will not run out"
> (cf. Ps. 102:25–27).

We can see several connections between this citation and things that the author will state in later chapters. The author will speak of the "shaking" of the created realm—its removal—in Heb. 12:26–27. Jesus Christ is "the same" yesterday, today, and *forever* in Heb. 13:8. Similarly, the author bases the effectiveness of Christ's high priesthood in Heb. 7 on his "indestructible life" (v. 16). While earthly priests die and cannot continue in their office, Christ always lives to intercede for the people (vv. 23–24). He remains a priest forever (v. 3).

Therefore, the focus of the psalm quotation in Heb. 1:10–12 is not on Christ's role as creator, but on the fact that he remains enthroned forever, unlike God's angel servants whose role is passing away. The angels are associated with a realm whose existence will soon come to an end. Yet Christ stands outside the created realm. These aspects of the quotation alone are enough to vindicate Caird's interpretation.

However, we can also make a good argument that the author is not even speaking literally of Christ as creator in these verses. For one thing, the author consistently speaks of *God* as creator of the world elsewhere in the epistle, as we noted in chapter 1. It is God who mends matter together to form the world in Heb. 11:3. Hebrews 2:10 even makes an implicit distinction between God as the one "through whom" the universe came to be and Christ as the son God perfected through sufferings. Only Heb. 1:3, which we showed has echoes of wisdom/*logos* language, refers to Christ as the one "through whom" God made the worlds. If creation was more about bringing order out of chaos than creation out of nothing, then certainly Christ's death is a creative event. It brings about new creation not only for God's people, but for the universe as well. It is thus fitting that the enthroned Christ be seen in creative terms vis-à-vis the creation.

Further, if the first three citations echo Christ's role as Son of God, the underlying theme of the entire catena, and if Heb. 1:8–9 implies the title of "Christ" in its reference to anointing, then Ps. 102:10–12 evokes the title "Lord." We showed earlier in the chapter that early Christian tradition looked to Jesus' exaltation as the point where he most meaningfully received these titles. Acts 2:34–35 aptly demonstrates the point:

> For David did not go up into the heavens, but he himself says, "The Lord said to my Lord, *sit at my right hand* until I place your enemies as a footstool for your feet." Therefore, let all Israel know with certainty that God *made him to be both Lord and Christ*, this Jesus whom you crucified.

The author of Hebrews inherited a tradition in which the title "Lord" could be applied to Jesus at the point of his enthronement as Son of God. This fact alone draws us away from a literal reading of the citation.

Hebrews 1:13

It is no coincidence that the passage we just read from Acts 2 includes a quotation of Ps. 110:1, for this verse was central to the early church's understanding of what it meant for Jesus to be Lord, Christ, and Son of God. Indeed, this verse may be the basis for Christians calling Jesus "Lord" in the first place.[32] We can safely say that it has been in the back of the author's mind the whole time. Allusions to it abound in Hebrews (e.g., 1:3, 13; 8:1; 10:13; 12:2).

> 13. And to which of the angels has he said at sometime,
> "Sit at my right hand until I place your enemies as a footstool for your feet"
> (cf. Ps. 110:1).

The way in which the author introduces this verse—"To which of the angels has he said at any time"—is exactly the same as the way in which he began the catena in 1:5. This literary device is called an *inclusio*, and it serves to bracket the catena by marking off its boundaries. It also serves to reinforce our claim that the catena has envisaged the exalted Christ all along, for the chain ends exactly where it began—with a clear reference to Christ enthroned at the right hand of God. The quotation from Ps. 2:7 began the catena with a reference to the exalted Christ; so Ps. 110:1 ends the chain with Christ enthroned, and it does so with the very verse to which the author alluded in Heb. 1:3 to launch the string of quotes.

> **inclusio** A way of binding a section of text together by beginning and ending it with similar words, phrases, or ideas.

If this observation did not demonstrate Caird's thesis beyond doubt, the association in early Christianity between Ps. 8 and Ps. 110:1 puts the nail in the coffin. Paul clearly connects the two psalms in 1 Cor. 15:25, as does Eph. 1:20–22.[33] We see that there is not nearly so great a disconnection between the ending of the catena in Heb. 1 and the argument of Heb. 2 as some have claimed. The two chapters constitute a fitting "narration" of the basic plot of salvation history up to the point where the audience of Hebrews is in the story. Such a background leads to the key verses of the epistle: Heb. 2:17–18. The author can thus start the thread of his main argument in 3:1.

CONCLUSION

Hebrews 1:5–14 is a kind of hymnic celebration of the exalted Christ that forms a fitting introduction to the epistle as a whole. The relevance of the catena to the rest of the epistle has not always been apparent to modern readers, but it would have been to the sermon's first audience. Early Christianity connected Ps. 110:1 and Ps. 8:4–6 as related perspectives on Christ's exaltation to the right hand of God. Christ was made lower than the angels when he took on human form and thus entered the domain in which angels ruled. On earth they guarded the appropriate standards of the law, and they ministered to God's people.

On the other hand, Christ's sinless death resulted in his coronation with glory and honor (Ps. 8:5), his seating at the right hand of God (Ps. 110:1). The early Christians saw this event as the point at which Jesus received the titles of "Lord," "Christ," and "Son of God," all of which are royal in nature. At this point he is postured for all things to be put under his feet (Ps. 8:6) and for his enemies to become his footstool (Ps. 110:1).

Therefore, while it may not appear so at first, the appropriate context against which to read the catena is the enthronement of Jesus as royal Son of God, Christ, and Lord. Not only is this indicated by the context, but the tradition histories of the individual citations themselves point to this interpretation. Finally, the broader context of the sermon as a whole shows how appropriate these verses are in introduction. Not only were angels associated with the old covenant, but to say Christ is now greater than the angels is to say that salvation is finally accomplished!

Chapter 4

Examples of Faith and Disbelief in the Old Covenant

INTRODUCTION

Hebrews is filled with contrasts and comparisons. A good number of the contrasts have to do with the Christology of the epistle—the author uses them to show his audience the superiority of Christ to various other figures from the old covenant. Christ is greater than Moses who gave the law. He is greater than any Levitical priest. His sacrifice and sanctuary are greater than the sacrifices and tabernacle of the old covenant. In general, he is God's new mediator to humanity, definitively replacing the angels. These contrasts primarily serve the exposition of Hebrews, the parts that are more theoretical/theological in orientation and of a somewhat "doctrinal" nature (e.g., Christ *is a greater* high priest than any Levitical priest).

However, a number of contrasts and comparisons serve the exhortations of Hebrews more directly, those passages that are more practical in orientation and intended to move the audience to take some course of action (e.g., do not be godless *like Esau* who sold his birthright). The author gives his audience both positive and negative examples that he either wishes them to imitate or avoid. The positive examples hold out potential for honor while the negative ones threaten shame.[1] The author brings up many characters from the story of salvation history strictly for this reason. They are examples of either faith or disbelief.

God's word is what these characters

> **Christology** The study of the person of Christ.
>
> **exposition** A genre whose primary orientation is toward deriving truths from the interpretation of Scripture.
>
> **exhortation** A genre whose primary orientation is toward moving the audience to take a course of action.

either believe or disbelieve. In the days of the old covenant, God spoke to the fathers through the prophets (Heb. 1:1). The author believes that much of what they had to say was about Christ. For example, Moses witnessed things that were "going to be spoken" through Christ (3:5; 1:2; 2:3). Hebrews 11 presents a long list of "heroes of faith" who believed in such promises even though they died before they came true. Nevertheless, they "saw them and greeted them from a distance" (11:13).

On the other hand, the generation of Israelites that came out of Egypt is a paradigm of disbelief in God's word. Their corpses fell in the desert as a result (3:17). The author hopes that these examples will bring the audience to reaffirm its commitment to the Christian message as he understands it.

GOD'S WORD IN THE OLD COVENANT

The Prophets and Scripture

The opening two verses of Hebrews mention that although God used to reveal himself to Israel through the prophets, he had now spoken definitively through a Son, Jesus Christ. Hebrews 2:3 clarifies that this more recent word through Christ was a message of salvation. Hebrews is basically a sermon designed to re-inspire its audience to persist in faithfulness to this message.

While speaking through Christ is a new way of speaking, Christ's message is not a radical departure from the previous message God gave through the prophets. The author of Hebrews believed that the message of those prophets was truly about Christ in the first place. We have already mentioned that Moses was a witness of the "things that were going to be spoken" through Christ (3:5). And while it would be inappropriate to continue to observe the Jewish law, Hebrews affirms the law's original validity—especially the way it foreshadowed what Christ would eventually do.

Hebrews argues as much or more from the Old Testament Scriptures as any other book in the New Testament. Indeed, it contains the longest Old Testament citation of any New Testament book (Heb. 8:8–12, quoting Jer. 31:31–34). Clearly its author considered the Old Testament Scriptures authoritative. The indefiniteness with which he occasionally introduces quotations highlights his sense that the Old Testament presents us with *God's* words rather than those of humans. Thus, while he probably believed that David had written the Psalms (cf. Heb. 4:7), he introduced Ps. 8 with the words, "*someone somewhere* has witnessed, saying." He never introduces Scripture in a way that looks to a human writer. It is rather consistently God (e.g., Heb. 1:5–7; 5:5–6; 10:37–38; 12:5–6), Christ (e.g., 2:12–13; 10:5–7), or the Holy Spirit (e.g., 3:7) that speaks the words of the Old Testament.

In keeping with the rest of the New Testament, the author of Hebrews often does not interpret Old Testament passages in terms of what they meant in their original contexts. In a few instances he could not have even made his point from the original Hebrew Scriptures—a telltale sign that the Bible he used was the Septuagint, the Greek translation of the Old Testament.[2] For example, in Heb. 9:16 he plays on the fact that the Greek word for "covenant" can also refer to a will. He could not have made such a point with the Hebrew word for covenant.

> **Septuagint** Although technically the Greek translation of the Pentateuch, the term is often used of the entirety of the Greek Old Testament used by Christians at the time of Christ.

Similarly, if one looks at Deut. 32:43 or Ps. 40:6, one will not find the words from which the author makes his points in Heb. 1:6 and 10:5. The words of the Old Testament he is using do not match up with the original words of the Hebrew Bible because of various changes that had taken place over the years as the text was passed on and later translated into Greek. This fact indicates that the author of Hebrews was a Greek speaker who probably did not know Hebrew or Aramaic.

The author reads the Old Testament through Christian eyes.[3] Rather than take the words in terms of what a human author might have understood them to mean, he places various Old Testament verses on the lips of God and Christ. They then take on the meaning such a divine and Christian context would imply.[4]

> **Compare:**
> "Sacrifice and offering you did not desire;
>   [but] *ears you opened* for me."
>   —Ps. 40:6
>
> "Sacrifice and offering you did not desire;
>   but a *body you prepared* for me."
>   —Heb. 10:5

For example, Ps. 40 was originally a prayer on the lips of one who was surrounded by troubles. The psalmist prays for rescue from impending murder. In the course of his lament, the author notes that what God wants from him is not sacrifice, but obedience. God wants his *ears* to be *open*.

On the other hand, Hebrews places these words on the lips of Christ as he is about to enter the world. Since he is using the words of the Greek Old Testament—words that speak of a *body* being *prepared* rather than ears being opened—the author can take them in a quite different way from what they originally meant. Now they mean that God no longer wants anyone anywhere to offer him sacrifices. Rather, the body God prepared for Jesus marks a transition from the old covenant to a new one. Such a meaning is far from what the psalm originally intended, but it helped further Hebrews's argument.

At other times the author looks to the story of the Old Testament as a foreshadowing of events and characters that relate to the age inaugurated by Christ.[5] For example, the settings of the Levitical cultus are "shadowy examples" of what Christ accomplishes through his death (cf. Heb. 8:5). Events that took place in the former age provide Hebrews's audience with pertinent examples for their own situation, such as the wilderness generation's failure to enter into God's promised land of rest (3:7–4:13).

Most important for this chapter, the period of the old covenant provides us with numerous characters that illustrate either faith or disbelief. While the godlessness of Esau is a notorious example of faithlessness to avoid, Heb. 11 presents a "cloud of witnesses" who had faith in God's promises even though they all died before receiving them (vv. 13, 39).

What unifies the word spoken through the prophets with that spoken through Christ is that both words have the same speaker, God. While Hebrews does not equate Christ with the "word" (*logos*) of God like John 1 does, it reflects some of the same currents in Judaism that saw God's word as the way he worked in the world. Hebrews 4:12 pictures God's word as a judge that discerns human intention, like a sword that could cleanly cut apart the inseparable. God's word (*hrema*) similarly mended the matter of the world into order (11:3) and is like the spirit of the heavenly realm (6:5).[6] Therefore, despite the contrast between the old and new covenants, God's ordering word provides continuity between both.

> To his archangelic and eldest *word* the father who gave birth to all things has freely given a special gift to stand in the middle and distinguish what has been created from the one who has created it. And this *word* is always a suppliant to the incorruptible one for the anxious mortal and an ambassador to the subject for the ruler.
> —Philo, *Her.* 205

The Certainty of God's Promises

The category of promise provided the author of Hebrews with another way of showing continuity between the revelations of the old and new covenants. Hebrews claims that God had always planned to atone for sins through Christ. Since in his view the audience is wavering in its Christian commitment, the author emphasizes the certainty of God's promises throughout the sermon. For example, he uses the case of Abraham both to show that God's promises are trustworthy and to provide a model for faith in them.

In Heb. 6:13–20, the author has just given a rather stern and foreboding warning to the audience concerning its dullness and the danger that it might "fall away" from the salvation offered through Christ (5:11–6:8). After this serious chiding, he then indicates his confidence that they will remain faithful to the Christian message (6:9–12). The remaining verses in the chapter reinforce the reasonableness of continuing in faithfulness by showing how God kept his promises to Abraham.[7]

The promise in question is God's statement that he will bless Abraham by giving him many descendants, a promise that the author notes has come to pass (6:15). It serves as a proof that God keeps his word. Two things in particular guarantee the certainty of this particular promise: (1) God swore it with an oath (6:17), and (2) God cannot lie (v. 18).[8]

In Heb. 7:20–25, the author points out that God took a similar oath with regard to Christ. In Ps. 110:4 God swears that Christ will be a priest forever. That verse even notes that God will never change his mind about such a switch in priesthood. The implication is that the Levitical cultus has definitively come to an end.

This imagery of oath taking goes along with the other language of sureness and certainty that pervades the epistle. The recurrence of words like "certain" (e.g., Heb. 2:2; 6:19), "make certain" (e.g., 2:3), "certainness" (6:16), "solid" (6:19), "anchor" (6:19), "boldness" (e.g., 4:16; 10:19), "remain" (e.g., 7:3, 24; 10:34; 12:27), and "hope" (e.g., 6:18; 7:19; 10:23) all create a sense of definitiveness to God's promises. It is no coincidence that Hebrews thinks of the final event in the plot in terms of what is "shaky" and what is unshakable. God will remove everything that is shakable, leaving only an unshakable kingdom (12:27–28).

Moses and the Law

We have mentioned several times that Moses witnessed the things going to be "spoken" through Christ. He did so as one of the prophetic voices of Heb. 1:1, as one of the instruments through whom the Scriptures were written. The author will build the heart of his argument in Hebrews 9–10 on the basis of texts from the Pentateuch, the Mosaic law. We can hardly underestimate the high regard with which Jews at the time of Christ held Moses.[9] Not only was he the one through whom God led Israel out of slavery in Egypt, but he was the one through whom God gave the law, one of the focal points of Second Temple Judaism.

As Jewish thought regarded angels as intermediaries between God and humanity, Jews considered Moses the most notable spokesperson for God in the Hebrew Scriptures. The author does not contrast Christ with Moses simply to show how great Christ was. The association between Moses and the law (which contained the legislation of the Levitical cultus) made it very appropriate to contrast the two. The author's discussion of Christ and Moses in Heb. 3:1–6 implicitly contrasts the two "covenants" with which these two individuals are associated. It foreshadows the later consideration of Christ as high priest, even though it takes a couple of chapters for the argument to get going in full force.

Hebrews 3:1–6 also includes themes from the arguments of the previous chapters, mainly the concentration on Christ as a Son. While Moses was faithful to God in the old covenant as a *servant*, Christ is faithful as a *Son* to the one who appointed him. It must have startled some in Hebrews's audience to hear its author say that Christ "has been deemed worthy of greater honor than Moses to the same degree that the one who builds a house has more honor than the house" (3:3)! Moses is thus both an example of faith in Hebrews and a foil against which the importance of Christ's high priesthood can be displayed. Just as the argument that follows in Heb. 3 shows that many of those under Moses' charge failed to enter into the promised land, so the author of Hebrews will hold out a warning to any under Christ's charge who do not persist until they enter into God's promised rest.

EXAMPLES OF DISBELIEF

The Wilderness Generation

For Hebrews, the paradigmatic example of disbelief is the generation of Israelites that left Egypt but never entered into the promised land of Canaan. The key to this failure was their lack of faith: "they were not able to enter in because of disbelief" (3:19). The author implies that the situation of the audience is quite similar. Like the wilderness generation, they too have left Egypt (v. 16). They have become enlightened and have partaken of holy spirit (6:4). They have partaken of the Christ (3:14), but they are in danger of not reaching the heavenly city in the end, the promised rest of God. Variations on this basic metaphor permeate the epistle and highlight the central point of the author's exhortations: persist on in your faithfulness to Christ.

First of all, the author's language throughout the epistle makes it clear that his audience has already joined the people of God and are "Christians" in the same sense that he is. His language in Heb. 5:11–6:8 presumes that they have repented, they have been baptized with water, and hands have been laid on them to represent the coming of the Holy Spirit. They have indeed partaken of holy spirit and have become enlightened. To use language from later in the epistle, they have arrived at the heavenly Jerusalem, and their spirits have been perfected and cleansed (12:22–24). Their sins have been taken away (10:10). In short, the community has experienced every Christian experience the author holds out to be a present possibility. We will discuss the community's history later in more detail, but suffice it to say that this group of Christians at one time were models of faith (cf. 6:9–12; 10:32–39).

The goal of the journey on which they have embarked is entrance into Canaan—God's promised land of rest. Scholars have sometimes debated over whether this promised rest is a present reality or a future hope. Some have wisely answered that it is both: "The 'rest', precisely because it is God's, is both present and future; men enter it, and must strive to enter it."[10] However, the most fundamental orientation of it for the author is toward its future dimension. It embodies the very reason why the author wishes his audience to continue on in faithful endurance.

Hebrews provides a number of images relating to the final goal of the Christian pilgrimage. In Heb. 3:7–4:13 it is Canaan, the intended destination of the wilderness generation. Psalm 95 included a plea to Israel not to rebel against God's will like those who left Egypt so many years before. After all, God took an oath that he would not allow those individuals into his rest, originally meaning the land of Canaan. In contrast, the author of Hebrews read the warning of the psalm as something the Holy Spirit was saying years after Israel entered Canaan. Joshua, he thought, must not have led Israel into the place of rest to which the Holy Spirit was referring in the psalm (Heb. 4:8). It is this prophesied rest that the author urges his audience to strive to enter.

As we just noted, the timing of Heb. 3:7–4:12 is somewhat ambiguous. These verses lend themselves both to the conclusion that the people of God can enter

God's rest currently and that it is still primarily future. Parallel images in the remainder of the epistle indicate that the focus of the rest is yet to come, yet it is also already present in some very important ways.

Probably the best parallel comes from Heb. 11, where the author speaks of Abraham as a stranger and pilgrim *on the earth* (v. 13). Like the wilderness generation, Abraham left his country for a place he did not know (v. 8). The patriarchs lived in tents (v. 9), portable dwellings like the tabernacle the author will argue from in Heb. 9–10. Abraham was looking for a city made by God, not by a human being (11:10), much as the sanctuary in which Christ serves was made by God and not human hands (8:2). Much as some in the wilderness generation longed to go back to Egypt, Abraham could have returned if he had so desired (11:15). Yet unlike the wilderness generation he had no desire to do so. Rather, he looked forward to a *heavenly* country, for the city God has prepared in *heaven* (v. 16). This destination is parallel to the promised rest of Heb. 3–4: Heaven is the focus of what the author understands the rest to be.

In keeping with Hebrews's pervasive contrast of the earthly with the heavenly, the rest to which he refers is associated with the heavenly realm. Abraham, of course, died without gaining access to that city (11:13). To some extent, the situation is changed for those who are in the new covenant. Since the possibility for our sins to be cleansed is a present reality, our spirits have already arrived at the heavenly Jerusalem in a sense (12:18–24). This aspect of Hebrews's thought constitutes the present possibility of entering God's rest.

Nevertheless, the rhetorical purpose for which the author tells the audience about the wilderness generation and Abraham is to urge them to shun the example of the first and emulate that of the second. In other words, the parallel of these illustrations in the life of the audience places the final rest as something still future, something they are still striving to enter "every day while it is called 'today'" (3:13). Hebrews 13:14 captures this fact aptly when it says, "We do not have here a city that remains but we are looking for the one that is coming." In other words, the focus of the rest is on the coming heavenly world of salvation (2:5) rather than on something pertaining to our current existence in this earthly realm.

The author uses the example of the wilderness generation to urge the audience of Hebrews to continue on in its pilgrimage toward this heavenly destination. He is afraid that "an evil heart of unbelief that turns from the living God" will arise among those in his audience (3:12). God has given them the promise of rest just as he did the Israelites in the desert (4:2), but it is only if we persist in the journey that we can truly consider ourselves covered by Christ's atonement (3:14). Those in the desert failed to enter God's rest because they did not hear the promise with ears of faith (4:2).

Esau

Hebrews is striking not only in its teaching that a Christian can "fall away" (6:6) and lose the benefit of Christ's sacrifice for sins (10:26). It also implies that once one has crossed such a fearful line, it is impossible to return (6:6). One of the most startling verses in the New Testament states that after Esau had sold his birthright, he "did not find a place of repentance even though he sought it with tears" (12:17). Given the nature of Hebrews's argument, its original audience must have found such a statement terrifying.

For the author of Hebrews, Esau is a model of someone who turns his or her back on Christ and then cannot find a way back. As was true of the audience, Esau was originally destined for inheritance as a son, but he sold that birthright for a single meal (12:16). In a sense, he prostituted himself to something other than his God. As we will argue in a subsequent chapter, the author intends this language to mirror the choices that currently stand before the audience.[11] Esau made the wrong choice. Later when he wanted to inherit the blessing, he was rejected (v. 17).

> "I had heard, sir," I said, "from certain teachers that there is not another repentance other than the one when we have gone down into the water and we have received the forgiveness of our former sins." He says to me, "You have heard well, for it is true."
> —Shepherd of Hermas Mand 4.3.1–2

Many Christian theological traditions find it difficult to process statements like these in Hebrews, although such statements are part of one particular debate among early Christians: Is there a "second repentance" for those who apostasize from the faith, particularly in times of persecution? In addition to the comments on Esau, two other passages in Hebrews teach the impossibility of return to Christ after apostasy.

The first and best known of these occurs in Heb. 6:4–6:

> It is impossible for those who once were enlightened, have tasted of the heavenly gift and become partakers of holy spirit, have tasted the good word of God and the powers of the coming age, and [then] have fallen away—it is impossible for them to come anew again to repentance, since they are crucifying the Son of God to themselves all over again and exposing him to public ridicule.

Many try to soften the import of this passage because of its implications. They might deny that the individuals in question were fully Christians before their fall or argue that this is merely a hypothetical situation that could never actually happen. Others emphasize the *present* tense of words like "coming anew" to repentance and "crucifying" the Son of God, suggesting that there might still be hope to return to Christ in the *future*. Yet none of these coping strategies really seems to work. The parallel with Esau makes it quite clear that Esau *wanted* to find a place of repentance, but could not find one. While we might find some solace in the particular nature of the audience's potential apostasy, we cannot interpret away the seriousness of this warning.

Hebrews 10:26–27 presents a similar admonition:

> If we continue sinning willfully after receiving the knowledge of the truth, the sacrifice for sins no longer remains but [rather] a certain fearful expectation of judgment and of a zealous fire about to eat [God's] enemies.

The audience must have found these words very sobering, especially since the author had just mentioned that Christ is waiting for his enemies to be placed under his feet (10:13).[12] The "sinning" mentioned here no doubt is another reference to the particular circumstances that gave rise to the epistle in the first place, circumstances that approach apostasy in the mind of the author.[13]

The author follows up this warning with another that uses an exegetical technique known as "from lesser to greater" (*a minore ad maiorem* or, in Hebrew, *qal wohomer*). The author starts by discussing the punishment of someone who rejected the law of Moses—the lesser example. Such an individual died without mercy on the basis of two or three witnesses (10:28). If that was the case, and the covenant instituted by Christ is even greater (cf. the similar argument in 2:2–3), then "how much greater a punishment do you think someone will deserve who tramples the Son of God under foot and deems the blood of the covenant unholy—the blood by which s/he was sanctified—and who insults the gracious Spirit?" (10:29). In the words of the text Jonathan Edwards made so well known: "It is a fearful thing to fall into the hands of the living God" (10:31).

> **qal wohomer** Literally "light and heavy," an exegetical technique that argues that if something is true of a lesser example, then it is certainly true of a greater one.

EXAMPLES OF FAITH

The Meaning of "Faith" in Hebrews

If the wilderness generation and Esau provided poignant examples of disbelief and faithlessness, Heb. 11 provided the audience with a great "cloud of witnesses" to faith.[14] Example lists such as the one found in that chapter are not uncommon in both Jewish and non-Jewish literature from this period.[15] Such lists bombarded their audience with a multitude of honorable (or dishonorable) individuals that implicitly encouraged the emulation (or avoidance) of their example. In Hebrews, the honorable individuals provided examples of faith and endurance in faith. They are typically persons who were persecuted for their righteousness, some of whom faced death as a consequence of faithfulness. Each example in its own way urges the audience to "run with endurance the race lying ahead" of them (12:1).

Many read Heb. 11, the "faith chapter" of the New Testament, in isolation from the rest of Hebrews. In particular, many Christians lift Heb. 11:1 out of its context and view it as some absolute definition of faith: "faith is the substance of that for which we hope, the verification of what is unseen." Here is another example of how chapter divisions sometimes obscure a book's train of thought. The verses that both immediately precede and immediately follow Heb. 11 provide us with extremely important clues to this chapter's meaning in Hebrews's world of thought.

> Faith is the substance of that for which we hope, the verification of what is unseen.
> —Heb. 11:1

Hebrews 10:19–39 come immediately after the author has finished his central argument: Christ has provided a definitive atonement once and for all; the Levitical system is now at an end. In consequence, he encourages his audience to approach God's heavenly throne with boldness (v. 19) and to hold fast their confession of faith on the basis of God's faithfulness to his promises (v. 23). He issues the stern warning we have just mentioned in the previous section: No sacrifice for sin remains if you apostasize (vv. 26–27).

Then the author uses the audience itself as an example of faith and endurance, a fact to which we will return later in the book.[16] In a former day, the audience had lost property and had associated themselves with the shame of Christians in prison. They had once had boldness like the author wants them to have now. Now they need endurance once again, he says (10:36). It will not be long before Christ comes (v. 37). Hebrews 10:39 asserts boldly the course the author believes the audience will indeed take: "we are not of the kind that shrink back into destruction but we are the kind that are faithful and obtain life."

The context of Heb. 11 thus indicates that the primary dimension of faith for Hebrews is that of endurance, faith*fulness*. David deSilva has recently pointed out the patron-client connotations of the word *faith* in Hebrews.[17] Ancient Mediterranean society functioned largely on the basis of rela-

patron–client relationships Informal arrangements by which those with resources (patrons) supplied those without (clients) in return for the honor and prestige they gained. In between the two parties often stood brokers that mediated such

tionships between those who had resources (patrons) and those who were in need of resources (clients).[18] Patrons supplied clients with their needs in return for the prestige they gained and the honor returned to them by those they supplied.

We should view in this light the relationship between God and humanity throughout the pages of the New Testament. All the gifts bestowed on humanity by God entail an obligation to "keep faith" with the giver. Faith thus involves not only a trust and belief in God as the giver but also faithfulness to him. It is thus possible to "break faith" with God, which would nullify the relationship. He would cease to act as patron.[19] The old faith/works debate is thus anachronistic and presents false alternatives. Faith, especially for a book like Hebrews, entails both faith and works as later Christians came to compartmentalize them.

The first few verses of Heb. 12 confirm that faithfulness or endurance is the focus of faith for the author. Given the cloud of witnesses from the example list in Heb. 11, the audience is encouraged to "lay aside every weight" and "the sin that easily causes entanglement" so that they can endure to the end of the race they are running (12:1). The author then gives Jesus as yet another example of endurance. In a sense he is the last example of someone in the old age that endured to the point of death (v. 2).

Therefore, "faith" in Hebrews is holding on and enduring, continuing in our journey toward the promised rest and the heavenly homeland. It is the substance now of the future things for which we hope (11:1). We already have the "beginning of substance," Heb. 3:14 says. We have already become partakers of holy spirit (6:4). Faith is holding onto that substance with endurance to the end.

The things for which we hope are not visible right now. Faith is the evidence we have now of those unseen things (11:1). The author illustrates faith as belief in the unseen by mentioning how God molded the *visible* world out of *invisible* things: "that which is seen has not come to exist out of things that appear" (v. 3). Noah built the ark because he trusted in what God had told him "about things that were not yet *seen*" (v. 7). Abraham set out on a journey even though he did not know where he was going and thus in a sense could not *see* the basis for what he was doing (v. 8). Moses also left Egypt and "endured as if he could see the *invisible*" (v. 27).

> The essence of faith in Hebrews is enduring in faithfulness because we trust in what God has promised, even though we do not visibly see any evidence that it is going to come true.

All these examples indicate that the essence of faith for the author's argument is enduring in faithfulness because we trust in what God has promised, even though we do not visibly see any real evidence that it is going to come true. No doubt the author crafted these specific examples in view of the situation of the audience as the author understood it. He believed that the audience was approaching a time of persecution in which their visible situation would not look too good. He wanted them to leave Egypt or rather to stay on their journey from Egypt, to journey into the unknown like Abraham, believing that they ultimately had a heavenly destination.

The Hall of Faith

We have already mentioned Heb. 11 several times in this chapter. This chapter provided the original audience with a "cloud of *witnesses*" to endurance and faithfulness. The author bound this chapter together through a technique called *inclusion* or *inclusio*—the chapter begins and ends with similar words and thoughts. Hebrews 11:2 states that because of their faith, "the elders were *witnessed*" or commended with honor. The second-to-last verse of the chapter also states, "All these, although they were *witnessed* [commended with honor] through faith, did not receive the promise," namely, the promise of atonement and salvation through Christ. The word *witness* binds the chapter together as a literary unit and indicates the basic thrust of the chapter.

The author has chosen these "witnesses" in particular because of the way each one specifically demonstrates faith. They are not generic examples of faithfulness. Rather, the author has chosen each individual in the light of the audience's situation. He carefully crafts the example list so that the honorable faith of the fathers (cf. Heb. 1:1) will inspire the audience in its current crisis.

The recurring allusions to death and resurrection are very noticeable in Heb. 11. It is reasonable to conclude that, at least in the mind of the author, the audience is facing a time of persecution that could involve martyrdom. The current situation requires them to consider themselves "strangers and aliens" in their place of residence (v. 13) and to ignore the laws of the land (cf. v. 23) upon threat of death. We will discuss whether the audience really did face such persecution later on in the book.[20]

In a momentary aside, the author gives a summary of the various examples he has discussed and tells the audience what he wishes them to gain from this "hall of faith." Hebrews 11:13 notes that "These all died in faith, even though they had not received the promises, but they saw them from afar and greeted them, confessing that they were strangers and aliens on the earth." This statement is similar to the one that concludes the chapter in verse 39. It is the chapter's bottom line. The author wishes the audience to know that they may very well die before they receive the promise. Indeed, they may very well die precisely because they are being faithful to God. Their here on earth may be a restless and uncomfortable one, like that of a stranger without a home. The honorable person remains faithful.

> Without faith it is impossible to please [God], for the one who comes to God must have faith that he exists and that he rewards those who seek him.
>
> —Heb. 11:6

Now some are delivered from death. Enoch was transformed so that he did not see death because he pleased God (11:5). Hebrews 11:32–34 tell how some actually won their battles (e.g., Gideon), shut the mouths of lions (e.g., Daniel), and escaped the flames (e.g., Shadrach, Meshach, and Abednego). Even after some had died, God raised them from the dead (v. 35—e.g., Elisha and the Shunammite woman).

However, the bulk of the examples in Heb. 11 relate to those who did not escape death, even if it was not a martyr's death. Abel's blood witnesses to a faith that endures even to death (11:4). Abraham's seed was as good as dead inside of him when God gave him the promise of Isaac (v. 12). Figuratively, Abraham receives Isaac back from the dead as he prepares to sacrifice him in faith (v. 19). With faith in future life, Isaac, Jacob, and Joseph all look forward to the future of Israel (vv. 20–22). While some escape martyrdom, "others were tortured and did not get released so that they might obtain a better resurrection" (v. 35, an apparent allusion to the Maccabean martyrs of 2 Macc. 7). All these examples seem calculated to defuse the threat of a martyr's death: You will rise from the dead even if you must die for your faith.

In keeping with potential persecution, a number of the examples seem to target the political/social situation of the audience. It is alienated in some way from its "city" and "country" (Heb. 11:14–16; 13:11–14). The example of Moses carries vague echoes of a "king's edict," suffering dishonor with God's people, and not fearing the king's wrath (11:23–27). Keeping faith with the invisible kingdom implies the judgment of the society around them, just as Noah's faith in building the ark condemned the world (v. 7), and the celebration of the Passover protected Israel from the coming wrath of God (v. 28). One has difficulty not seeing in "Egypt" and "Jericho" echoes of some political establishment in the life of the audience (vv. 29–30), and in the faith of Rahab we have an echo of the faithlessness of the wilderness generation, here implicitly compared to those in the audience who are abandoning their faith because of the current crisis (v. 31).

The promise for which all these characters of the story awaited was the promise of perfection provided through Christ (11:40). Like the audience, they looked forward to the heavenly city, the coming world of salvation. Like the audience, their visible circumstances were often not commensurate with their faith. Nevertheless, they still died in faithfulness to God. As such, they continue to serve as a cloud of honorable witnesses that can inspire us to endurance.

Jesus

Christians today often do not think of Christ as a model of faith. For some, even to suggest such a thing takes away from his divinity. Nevertheless, the early Christians had no problem "looking to Jesus" as an example for them to emulate and follow. In the plot of salvation history, Jesus stands as the final example of someone in the old age who was faithful to the point of death, even though his death and exaltation inaugurated the new age.

After the author has given his list of faithful examples in Heb. 11, he goes on to encourage his audience to look to Jesus' example as well. Jesus was the "founder and perfecter of faith, who because of the joy set before him endured the cross, despising shame" (12:2). Hebrews urges its audience to observe how he behaved when he encountered the opposition of sinners and then follow his example (v. 3).

Many Christians find it startling to read about how God "perfected" Christ (e.g., Heb. 2:10; 5:9). Hebrews 5:8 similarly states that "although [Jesus] was a son, he learned obedience from the things he suffered." Such a comment is sometimes difficult to understand in the light of whom Christians believe Christ to be. After all, Hebrews itself refers to Christ as "God" (1:8). In part such statements startle us because we do not properly understand the original connotations of the words and in part because we do not fully understand why the author says them in the first place.

The issue of perfection is difficult because we often think of the word in terms of morality, with the implication that a lack of perfection is sinfulness or inadequacy.[21] We also tend to see it as a matter of being the "best," and thus we cannot understand how Christ could ever be considered anything less. The word for perfection in Greek is basically about *completeness*, though, rather than morality or infinite quality. The completeness of both Christ and humanity in the plot comes with the attainment of glory and honor.[22] The attainment of God's intended glory in the heavenly realm thus stands in the background of perfection language in the epistle.

For humans, perfection does have a moral component, for a human being cannot attain the most appropriate and "complete" human status unless his or her sins have been cleansed. Without such a cleansing we are incomplete humanity, "imperfect" humanity. Sin is the very thing keeping us from our intended glory. Human perfection in Hebrews is thus closely associated with the cleansing of one's conscience (cf. the parallelism of 10:1–2), although it also has overtones of reaching heaven (e.g., 12:23).

For Christ, perfection has no moral component, since he is without sin. His goal is to attain glory and lead many sons to glory. He is thus perfected when he has demonstrated appropriate obedience on earth (cf. 5:7), suffered on behalf of his brothers (e.g., 2:10; 5:9), and been exalted to God's right hand (e.g., 7:28). Perfection for Christ implies that he has successfully completed the human experience and appropriately been exalted to glory in the heavenly realm.

Other misunderstandings come from the statement that Jesus "learned obedience" (5:8). We find it hard to imagine how someone would need to learn obedience unless he or she had been disobedient. Such is, of course, not the case with Christ, who was without sin (4:15). Whatever it might mean to learn obedience, it does not imply that Jesus had been disobedient.

It is important to realize that the author makes this statement about Jesus learning obedience as much with a view to the audience as with a view to Christ. As Jesus was a son who learned obedience, the audience is also made up of "sons" who are currently undergoing a kind of "discipline." In other words, the author holds Christ up once again as an example for the audience to emulate. In the days of his flesh he also had a struggle with death. He prayed with "strong crying and tears" to the one whom he knew could rescue him out of the grave (5:7). Like Noah who in godly reverence built the ark (11:7), so Christ showed godly fear (5:7). As the Philippian hymn put it, he was obedient to death, even death on a cross (Phil. 2:8). God "heard" his prayer accordingly, and he became a cause of salvation to those who obey him (Heb. 5:7, 9).

> Human perfection in Hebrews is closely associated with the cleansing of one's sins, especially since this implies that one will attain to glory in the heavenly realm.
>
> Perfection for Christ implies his successful, sinless completion of the human experience and the subsequent attainment of glory as he is exalted to God's right hand.

The audience must therefore endure God's discipline just as Christ faithfully endured sufferings.[23] The word *discipline* often has a punitive sense in the way we use it, and God is indeed punishing the audience to some extent with their trials (12:6). Yet the discipline God is meting out to the audience of Hebrews has as much to do with strengthening them and helping them *become disciplined* as it does with punishment. God is training them as he does everyone, even Jesus (12:8; 5:8).

God is training them for their own benefit so that they can partake of God's holiness (12:10). Ancient fathers disciplined their children (v. 7), yet such children respected their fathers "of flesh" for disciplining them. How much more will the audience *live* if they respect the "father of spirits" (v. 9). The example of Jesus as a son who faithfully "learned obedience" in the time of his suffering stands out to the audience as the supreme example of faith and endurance.

CONCLUSION

Many of the characters in the plot of salvation history serve as examples of either faith or disbelief to God's word. Like such individuals, the audience of Hebrews had also received God's word and thus faced the same choice of either faith or faithlessness. The wilderness generation provided them with a paramount example of individuals who started out on a journey toward God's promise but failed to attain it because of their disbelief. Esau also started out with a birthright. He was a son on his way to receive an inheritance, but his godless unfaithfulness lost it for him. Then when he wished to regain it, he could not find a place of repentance.

Such examples provided sobering warnings to the audience of Hebrews. Like the wilderness generation and Esau, they had left Egypt and had a promise of inheritance extended to them. The author sternly warns them that their corpses could also fall in the desert, and they might also find their birthright irreparably lost. Endurance in faith was the key to inheritance.

The great cloud of witnesses in Heb. 11 provided more honorable examples. These were individuals who continued on their journey toward the promise even though they all died without receiving it. They endured because they could see beyond the visible to the invisible, to the heavenly homeland toward which they were ultimately striving. None of them viewed death as the final word but looked beyond it to the promise of life, even when it meant shame and persecution by the political and social forces around them.

The same God who had spoken formerly to these faithful fathers through the prophets had also spoken a sure promise of salvation to the audience through Jesus. This salvation through Jesus was in fact that to which Moses and the prophets were ultimately testifying about anyway. Jesus himself provided the ultimate example of a son who learned obedience through the things he suffered. The author encouraged his audience to look to Jesus' example and imitate his faithfulness.

Chapter 5

A Better Sacrifice, Sanctuary, and Covenant

INTRODUCTION

Christ is the main character in the story of "salvation history." This term, *salvation history*, refers to the story of how God has liberated sinful humanity from the power of death and enabled us to obtain the glory he intended us to have from the very beginning. God has made this glory possible through Christ. By his sinless death Christ destroyed the devil and is now leading many sons to glory.

Chapter 2 presented the resolution of the plot of salvation in two stages: (1) Christ defeats the devil's power over death by offering himself as an atoning sacrifice, and (2) God removes the created realm and everything in the universe that is "shakable." This chapter deals with the first of these two stages.

The author of Hebrews inherited much of his Christology—his understanding of Jesus Christ—from those who were Christians before him. For example, it seems likely that he knew some of the apostle Paul's teaching. We briefly discussed a few of these similarities in chapter 2. Both Paul and the author of Hebrews seem to have considered Christ a "second Adam." Both used Ps. 8 to show not only that humanity has "fallen short" of the glory of God but also to show what Christ has done for us.

Hebrews also echoes the earlier Christian notion that Christ's death was a sacrifice for sins. For instance, Rom. 8:3 refers to Christ's death as a sin offering like those prescribed in Lev. 4. Paul may even compare his death to the sacrifice offered on the Day of Atonement (Rom. 3:25), a sacrifice made only once a year.[1] Further, in 1 Cor. 5:7 Paul compares Christ's death to a Passover lamb, the lamb that in Exod. 12 kept the death angel away from the firstborn sons of the Israelites. All of these images indicate that Paul understood Christ's death to atone for the sins of those who had faith in him.

One of the most significant debates Paul had with other Jewish Christians was whether faith in Christ was sufficient in and of itself to make a Gentile acceptable to God on the day of judgment.[2] Although Paul's writings do not discuss this issue in terms of atonement, his argument raises the question of whether Christ's death was sufficient in and of itself to atone for one's sins.[3] For example, Paul never said that the sacrificial system in Jerusalem had become outdated or that Christians should not sacrifice at it. In fact, the temple-favoring author of Luke–Acts pictures Paul offering a sacrifice in the temple near the end of his life (Acts 21:24).

> **atonement** The reconciliation of humanity to God made by way of sacrifice or some offering in order to make amends.
>
> **sin offering** One of the five basic offerings prescribed by Leviticus (Lev. 4), its purpose was to provide atonement for unintentional sins one might commit (sins committed in ignorance).
>
> **Day of Atonement** Yom Kippur, the one day a year when the high priest entered into the innermost room of the sanctuary (the Holy of Holies or Most Holy Place). The high priest atoned for all the sins of the people on this day (cf. Lev. 16; Num.

In this sense, the book of Hebrews goes one step beyond Paul's writings in its attitude toward the Jewish sacrificial system. For Paul, we disgrace Christ if we think something more than his death is needed to reconcile us to God. For Hebrews, it is apostasy to rely in any way on the Old Testament sacrificial system for atonement. Christ's death atoned for all the sins of the world and rendered the entirety of the Jewish sacrificial system obsolete.

To accomplish this rhetorical purpose, Hebrews pits Christ against the entirety of the Old Testament cultus through an extended metaphor based on the Day of Atonement. While this once-a-year event atoned for the sins of the people for that one year, Hebrews will argue that Christ's onetime death potentially atoned for all the sins of everyone that ever has or will live for all time. The earthly cultus of the Old Testament covenant consisted of Levitical priests offering perpetual sacrifices in an earthly sanctuary. Hebrews will propose a "new covenant" based on Christ as a heavenly high priest offering himself once and for all in a heavenly sanctuary.

Using quasi-Platonic language, the author argues that the operations of the Levitical sacrificial system were only shadowy examples of the true atonement Christ would ultimately provide. In this way he can show not only that Christ has definitively replaced any need for Levitical atonement, but he can also argue that continued reliance on such means of atonement constitutes apostasy from Christ. The author's exposition thus serves as the basis for his exhortations for the audience to persist in their faithfulness to Christ over and against some "old covenant" element in their current situation. God never expected the Old Testament cultus actually to take away sins.

CHRIST, MEDIATOR OF A BETTER COVENANT

The New Covenant

As the prophet Jeremiah mourned the destruction of Jerusalem, he bemoaned the fact that the people of his day were suffering for the sins of a previous generation. The saying was going around that "the fathers ate the sour grape, but the teeth of the sons rotted" (Jer. 31:29). It is in this context that the books of Jeremiah and Ezekiel proclaim that God will take a different tactic in the future: the person who actually does the sinning will be the one who dies (Jer. 31:30; Ezek. 18:4).

Jeremiah goes on to speak of a *new covenant* that God will make with his people, unlike the previous one. He says that those under this covenant will not need to teach one another how to keep God's law, for "days are coming" when God will put his laws inside his people, writing them on their hearts and minds (Jer. 31:33–34). With the law inside them, everyone will know the Lord. In those last days, God will forgive their wickedness and no longer remember their sins.

The author of Hebrews believed that such days had finally arrived with the coming of Christ. Although God formerly spoke through the prophets, "in these last days" he had spoken through a Son (Heb. 1:1–2). The phrase "these last days" not only echoes the prophecies of the book of Jeremiah, but the word "these" indicates that the new covenant has actually arrived through Christ. The days that *were* coming have finally come.

The idea of a new covenant was not new with Hebrews.[4] Even before Jesus, some Dead Sea Scrolls spoke of a new covenant. For them, this new covenant involved the arrival of a human messiah who would rule over a restored Israel, not to mention a legitimate priest who would preside over the correct observance of the law.[5] Jesus himself may have taught the arrival of a new covenant. Both Luke and Paul present Jesus' death as the inauguration of a new covenant on the basis of Jesus' blood (Luke 22:20; 1 Cor. 11:25). As we might expect, however, Paul comes closest to Hebrews when he writes that those in Christ have the Spirit inside them and are thus part of a "new covenant" based on the Holy Spirit and not on the Jewish law (2 Cor. 3:6). Echoing Jer. 31, Paul implies that the one who is in Christ has the law written on his or her heart by way of the Holy Spirit.

Hebrews takes this image much further than Paul's writings and in a drastically different direction from that of the Dead Sea Scrolls. When Hebrews speaks of the new covenant, it envisages the end of the Old Testament sacrificial system, which it virtually equates with the Jewish law. In the longest Old Testament citation in the New Testament, Hebrews quotes Jer. 31 in

> When [God] speaks of a "new" covenant, he has made the first covenant old. And the covenant that is aging and growing old is near its disappearance.
>
> —Heb. 8:13

order to proclaim an end to the old covenant mediated through Moses and the angels.

The sacrificial system of the Old Testament is thus the heart of what Hebrews means by the "old covenant," just as Hebrews primarily refers to the Levitical cultus when it speaks of the "law."[6] It is no surprise that after the author proclaims the disappearance of the old covenant, he goes on to contrast Christ's sacrifice with those offered by Levitical priests. Hebrews 7:11 similarly states that the law was put into effect on the basis of the Levitical priesthood. The author argues that since God has instituted a new kind of priesthood through Christ, he has changed the law as well (7:12)—even canceled it (v. 18).

> "Days are coming," says the Lord, "when I will bring into effect with the house of Israel and with the house of Judah a new covenant, not like the covenant I made with their fathers on the day when I took them by their hand to lead them out of Egypt. They did not remain in my covenant and I rejected them," says the Lord. "This covenant that I will make with the house of Israel after those days," says the Lord, "will give my laws on their minds and write them on their hearts. I will be their God and they will be my people. Each will not teach his neighbor and his brother saying, 'Know the Lord,' for all will know me from smallest to greatest. I will be gracious toward their unrighteous deeds and will no longer remember their sins."
> —Heb. 8:8–12, citing Jer. 31:31–34

Scholars have often missed the connections between Hebrews's contrast of the two covenants and some of the other contrasts in the epistle. For example, the contrast of Christ with the angels in Heb. 1 is essentially about the fact that Christ has replaced the angels as God's mediator to his people. God no longer needs angels as intermediaries to the earth in the new covenant since the created realm is about to be removed anyway (12:27).

Similarly, the contrast between Christ and Moses in Heb. 3 is not made simply to show how great Christ is in general. Hebrews 8 specifically contrasts Christ with Moses as the mediator of a better "law" than the one Moses mediated. Christ "has now obtained a more excellent ministry [than Moses], inasmuch as he is the mediator of a better covenant that has been enacted as law on the basis of better promises" (8:6; compare 7:11). The law that Moses inaugurated "perfected nothing" (7:19). On the other hand, Christ's covenant can actually take away sins (10:14).

The central argument of Hebrews shows that the sacrifices of the Levitical system did not actually take away sin. Rather, they were shadowy examples that looked forward to the time when Christ, with one offering, would take away sins forever (8:5; 10:4). As the author of Hebrews came to the end of his central argument, he punctuated his claim with a recap of Jer. 31. God promised to write his laws on their hearts and no longer to remember their sins (Heb. 10:16–17). Since God's new covenant in Christ has accomplished this forgiveness, all sacrifices for sins have come to an end (v. 18). The Levitical sacrificial system is no longer valid.

Christ, Greater than the Angels

In one of the places where Philo mentions angels, he refers to them as "emissaries from humanity to God and from God to humanity" (*Gig.* 16).[7] The author of Hebrews no doubt also believed that the angels were mediators between God and humanity in general, but they had another function that was even more important for him. For the author of Hebrews, angels were the operative ministers to God's people under the old covenant. They were "ministering spirits sent for those about to inherit salvation" (Heb. 1:14). Therefore, for Hebrews the contrast between Christ and the angels is a part of the contrast between the two covenants.[8]

When the author of Hebrews argues that Christ has become greater than the angels, he indicates that Christ is now the appropriate way to gain access to God's presence. Those whom the angels served as intermediaries were located on the earth under the power of death and the devil—but that same earth will be "rolled up like a garment" (1:12) when God's unshakable kingdom arrives (12:28). Moreover, while the angels were the channel through which God spoke the law to Moses (2:2), God has spoken a superior and definitive word of salvation through Christ that makes the angelic word obsolete (v. 3).

Christ, Greater than Moses

Hebrews 3:1–6 contrast Christ and Moses.[9] While Moses was faithful as a servant in God's house, Christ was faithful as a Son (vv. 5–6). Christ thus has as much greater glory than Moses as the builder of a house has more honor than the house itself (v. 3). Indeed, the true meaning of Moses' faithfulness was his witness to Christ (v. 5), since the true purpose of the law revealed through Moses was to foreshadow what Christ himself did in the end (8:5).

Therefore, the contrast between Christ and Moses relates directly to the contrast between the two covenants as well. Moses was a witness of the "things that would be spoken" through Christ (cf. 1:2; 2:3). When God told Moses to "be careful to make everything according to the type shown you on the mountain," God was giving him a "shadowy example" of the heavenly ministry Christ would accomplish (8:5). When Heb. 8:6 speaks of Christ as the mediator of a better covenant "that has been enacted as law [*nenomothetetai*] on the basis of better promises," the author deliberately contrasts Christ's new covenant with what he has said previously of the Mosaic law. While "the people have been given the Law [*nenomothetetai*] on the basis of the Levitical priesthood" (7:11), Christ has effected a new priesthood and a new "law."

CHRIST, A GREATER PRIEST

If the author is going to contrast Christ with the entirety of the Old Testament sacrificial system, he must demonstrate three things: (1) that Christ is a superior priest to the Levitical priests, (2) that Christ offers a superior sacrifice to the old covenant sacrifices, and (3) that Christ offers this sacrifice in a superior sanctuary to any of the sanctuaries of the Old Testament. In the central chapters of Hebrews the author will argue all three of these points.

Hebrews 5 and 7 are where the author argues that Christ is a superior priest to any Levitical priest. While it has proved very difficult for scholars to agree on the precise literary structure of Hebrews, it is fairly clear that a transition of some significance takes place near the beginning of Heb. 5.[10] Up to this point, the author's argument has focused largely on Christ as a Son. Hebrews 5:5 in fact recapitulates an Old Testament citation that appeared in Heb. 1: "You are my Son; today I have given you birth" (Heb. 1:5). However, from this point on in the argument the focus shifts from Christ's sonship to his priesthood. Another statement from God to Christ provides the keynote for the chapters that follow: "You are a priest forever after the order of Melchizedek" (5:6).

The Order of Melchizedek

Psalm 110:1 is one of the most important Old Testament texts for Hebrews, in fact for the very foundations of New Testament Christology: "The LORD said to my Lord, 'Sit at my right hand until I make your enemies a footstool for your feet.'"[11] The author not only quotes this verse in Heb. 1:13, he alludes to it four other times in the epistle (1:3; 8:1; 10:12; and 12:2). The prominence of the psalm is so great in Hebrews, that one scholar has gone so far as to suggest that Hebrews was a sermon based on Ps. 110, delivered on the day when that psalm was the synagogue reading.[12]

However, while Ps. 110:1 plays a role in many other places in the New Testament, Hebrews is the only New Testament writing that explicitly mentions Ps. 110:4: "The LORD took an oath and will not regret it, 'You are a priest forever after the order of Melchizedek.'" Hebrews claims that Christ is this kind of priest. This verse allowed the author to consider Christ as a heavenly priest as well as a king, a high priest in a heavenly sanctuary.

It is difficult to know whether it was the author of Hebrews himself who first thought of Christ as a high priest. Paul seems to picture Christ in a priestly role in Rom. 8:34 where he intercedes for us. Interestingly, Christ performs this intercession "at God's right hand"—an allusion to Ps. 110:1. It may very well be that Ps. 110:4 stands behind Paul's comments here and that Paul also thought of Christ as a priest.

On the other hand, Hebrews sees Jesus as a *high* priest in parallel to the earthly high priest on the Day of Atonement. While in Rom. 3:25 *God* offers Christ as an atoning sacrifice, in Hebrews Christ is both the offering *and the one who offers*, both high priest *and* sacrifice. The difficulty of picturing such an event indicates the highly metaphorical nature of the author's imagery. We need to be very careful to distinguish between what the author means literally and what is metaphor.[13]

Numerous scholars have advanced hypotheses to explain the appropriate background behind the author's use of Melchizedek in Heb. 7.[14] In general, we can distinguish two basic approaches: those that see him as a literal being and those that see him as a literary foil.

In the wake of the Dead Sea Scrolls, many were excited to find a fragment that seemed to make reference to an angelic being named Melchizedek who was involved in the judgment of the world (11QMelch). Understandably, it was not long before some suggested that the Melchizedek of Heb. 7 was this same being.[15] The later gnostic literature also had a place for Melchizedek among the heavenly host. For those who see the category of the angelic as central to the development of the early Christian understanding of Christ, an angelic Melchizedek in Heb. 7 would support their case.

All such hypotheses are implausible, however, because the author never argues for the superiority of Christ over Melchizedek, as he does with angels in general in Heb. 1. If the author's description of Melchizedek referred to a real person—"without father, without mother, without genealogy, neither having beginning of days nor end of life" (7:3)—the author would surely have needed to show that Christ was even greater still.[16] Melchizedek is conspicuous in Hebrews's argument precisely because the author does not see a need to contrast Christ with him even though he lived during the time of the old covenant.

In reality, one cannot understand the author's argument in Heb. 7 appropriately unless one keeps in mind that it is an interpretation of the phrase, "a priest after the order of Melchizedek." The author wished to clarify for his audience what God meant when he said that the Christ would be a priest after the order of Melchizedek. Understandably, he turned to the only other *text* in the Old Testament where Melchizedek is mentioned, namely Gen. 14. In other words, the author used the *text* of Gen. 14 to interpret the phrase "order of Melchizedek" in the *text* of Ps. 110:4. He primarily had a view to the Melchizedek of the text rather than to the Melchizedek of history.[17]

With this fact in mind, it is no surprise that the author begins his explication of the Melchizedekian priestly order with an allegorical interpretation of the text of Gen. 14:17–20. Reasoning from the etymology of the words, the author takes the name "Melchizedek" to mean "king of righteousness," and the phrase "king of Salem" to mean "king of peace." The author makes these interpretations because they help define what a priest after the order of Melchizedek is. Christ is indeed a righteous, sinless king who brings peace.

The author goes on to interpret the Genesis passage further. As far as the text is concerned, Melchizedek is "without father, without mother, without genealogy, neither having beginning of days nor end of life" (Heb. 7:3). It has been all too easy to take this verse out of context as a freestanding comment on the person of Melchizedek or Christ.[18] One will not properly understand the statement, however, unless one keeps in mind (1) that it is in reference to priesthood not personhood, and (2) that it is an interpretation of the *text* of Gen. 14, not the historical individual Melchizedek.

As a priest, the Melchizedek of the text had no priestly father or mother. He had no priestly genealogy at all, no human lineage that would lead one to think of him as a priest. Indeed, Heb. 7:6 mentions again the fact that Melchizedek did not trace his priestly genealogy from Levi. Genesis also provides no record of him beginning or ending the days of his priestly service, just as it does not narrate his birth or death. In short, the text of Genesis is silent about his parentage, priestly origins, birth, and death.

> **non in thora non in mundo** A Jewish exegetical technique based on the idea that if the Torah was silent about something, then that thing could be considered not to exist for interpretive purposes.

The silence of the Genesis text allowed the author to use an exegetical technique known as *non in thora non in mundo*: "If it is not in the law, it does not exist." For interpretive purposes, we can say that a priest after the order of Melchizedek has no priestly lineage, no point at which he takes over from another priest or surrenders his office to someone who will succeed him. Most important of all for the author, a priest after the order of Melchizedek has no end of life, just as the death of Melchizedek is not narrated in Genesis.

The never-ending quality of Christ's priesthood is one of the most important reasons why it succeeds where the Levitical priests failed. A priest after the likeness of Melchizedek does not serve in accordance with the "fleshly" oriented commandments of the Levitical sacrificial system. Rather, a Melchizedekian priest serves on the basis of the power of an indestructible life (Heb. 7:16). Unlike the countless Levitical priests whose service is severely limited by their own eventual deaths, Christ remains forever with an indestructible priesthood (v. 24). In a statement reminiscent of Rom. 8:34, Hebrews notes that Christ always lives to intercede for those who come through him to God, presumably in reference to the forgiveness of their sins (Heb. 7:25).

Therefore, in terms of what a Melchizedekian priest actually is, *Christ is the only one who has ever been or will ever be such a priest.* Ironically, not even the historical Melchizedek himself was truly in the order; God simply used what the Scripture said of him to foreshadow Christ. Scripture "likened" him to the Son of God who truly remains a priest forever (7:3). Christ is thus a priest after the order of Melchizedek because he lives and stands in heaven as a cause of eternal salvation (5:9–10). The "order" of his priesthood is a heavenly one, not an earthly one (8:4).

Christ's Appointment to the Order

Hebrews 5 lays out the essential characteristics of priesthood. According to Heb. 5:1, high priests are appointed to offer gifts and sacrifices to God for sins (see also Heb. 8:3). You become a priest by divine appointment: You cannot become one just because you want to (5:4). The key function of priesthood is intercession to

God for his people. As he intercedes, a high priest sympathizes with the weakness and ignorance of the people, for he has weaknesses as well (v. 2). Such earthly high priests must offer sacrifices for their own sins before they sacrifice for the people (5:3; 7:27–28; 9:7).

Christ's high priestly résumé not only meets these qualifications; it surpasses them. Just as the call of Aaron and the Levitical priests came in accordance with their lineage, God appoints Christ on the basis of his resurrection/exaltation. The same God who pronounced Jesus to be "Son" at his exaltation also pronounced him to be a priest after the order of Melchizedek at that time (Heb. 5:5–6). As God perfects Christ, he appoints him as a priest after the order of Melchizedek (vv. 9–10). Superior to the earthly priests, he serves in the true sanctuary in heaven (8:2–4; 9:11).

Like other priests, he also sympathizes with the trials of those for whom he intercedes. God made him human in every way so that he could become a faithful and merciful high priest (2:17). He was tempted in every way that other humans are, yet he showed his priestly superiority in that he did not have sins of his own to cleanse (4:15). Yet he underwent the same trials as humanity in general, so he can help those like the audience who undergo testing (2:18).

Jesus' suffering of death provides us with the greatest example of such a trial. Because of his faithfulness to God, Jesus faced the possibility of death (cf. 5:8). Like a priest, he offered prayers and supplications to God in the time of his trial with "strong crying and tears" (v. 7). This cry probably was his plea to God for salvation out of the realm of death—a prayer that God heard because of Christ's godliness (v. 7). After he had offered one sacrifice for all time, his priestly work brought about eternal salvation for all who avail themselves of it (v. 9). Unencumbered by death, his sacrifice remains valid forever (6:20; 7:28; 10:14).

If we press the details of Christ's high priesthood too far, we begin to run into difficulties. Questions like when exactly Christ became a high priest, what exactly he offered, where he offered it and when—Hebrews gives us data at various points that could lead us to quite different conclusions on these issues. These tensions derive from the fact that Christ's high priesthood is basically metaphorical in nature. When we take the imagery too literally, the metaphors break down.

The Superiority of the Melchizedekian Order over the Levitical

Hebrews 7:1–3 uses Gen. 14 to interpret what it might mean to be a "priest after the order of Melchizedek." Reading that text allegorically, the author concludes that the order of Melchizedek relates to Christ as a righteous king-priest who has no priestly lineage but whose service is unending because he never dies. The middle section of Heb. 7 goes on to show not only that such a priesthood is superior to the Levitical priesthood but that God's appointment of Christ as this kind of priest entails the end of the Levitical priesthood as a whole.

Continuing this interpretation of Gen. 14, Heb. 7:4–10 focuses on the verses where Abraham gives tithes to Melchizedek and Melchizedek blesses Abraham

(Heb. 7:1–2). The author argues that this event shows that Melchizedek is greater than Abraham, for only a greater can bless a lesser and naturally it is the lesser who gives tithes to the superior (vv. 6–7). Moreover, because Levi was Abraham's great-grandson, we can say in a sense that Levi also offered tithes to Melchizedek while he was still in the loins of Abraham (vv. 9–10). The conclusion was obvious to the author of Hebrews: A Melchizedekian priest is greater than a Levitical priest.

A priest in the order of Melchizedek is also superior to earthly priests because such a priest has an indestructible life (7:16) and a permanent priesthood (v. 24), always living to intercede for those who approach God for cleansing (v. 25). The silent witness of the Genesis text indicates that Melchizedek lives, while Levitical priests die regularly (v. 8). Interestingly, Hebrews does not make much connection between Christ as a Melchizedekian priest and his sacrificial death. Certainly his atoning death is a presupposition for his heavenly priesthood, but the author connects the order of Melchizedek strictly to Christ's exalted life beyond death. Here is another reminder of the highly metaphorical and rhetorical nature of the author's argument.

Hebrews 7:11–19 goes on to show that the arrival of a Melchizedekian priest entails an end to the Levitical priesthood. The author argues that the law was put into effect on the basis of the Levitical priesthood. If perfection had been possible by this means, however, no Melchizedekian priest would have ever arisen (v. 11).[19] For Christ to become a priest means that the law must be changed, for Christ is not from the appropriate tribe to be a priest according to the law (vv. 12–14). The need for the law to be changed is even clearer since Christ is a priest in the superior order of Melchizedek (v. 15). God's appointment of Christ as such a priest, verified definitively with an oath, indicates the "cancellation of the preceding command because of its weakness and uselessness" (v. 18). In Christ, God introduces a better hope (v. 19).

A BETTER SACRIFICE AND SANCTUARY

We began the preceding section by mentioning three things that the author needed to argue in order to contrast Christ with the entirety of the Old Testament sacrificial system. We just finished the first of these, namely, the author's argument that Christ is a greater priest than any earthly, Levitical priest. The other two things the author wished to show were (1) that Christ offered a more effective sacrifice than the sacrifices of the old covenant, and (2) that he offered it in a superior sanctuary. Hebrews 9–10 will argue both of these things.

At first glance, the author's discussion of the superior sacrifice and sanctuary of the new covenant might seem straightforward. A sanctuary exists in heaven that is the true sanctuary, and Christ entered into its Holy of Holies after dying on the cross for our sins. The earthly sanctuary was in fact modeled after the heavenly one so that its sacrifices would foreshadow the real sacrifice Christ would eventually offer (see Fig. 7). The Levitical system was never meant to be permanent and never actually took away sins—it was an illustration of what was to come. Now that Christ has brought about a true sacrificial cleansing, all Levitical priests and sacrifices are obsolete, as well the earthly sanctuary.[20]

The problem is that almost every aspect of the preceding summary breaks down if it is taken as a literal picture and pursued in detail. For example, it is important for Hebrews that Christ be a *heavenly* high priest (8:4) who offers himself in a *heavenly* sanctuary (9:11). Yet the author can also indicate that Christ's sacrifice was his *body* (10:10) offered *when he died* (9:27–28). These latter comments would place Christ's high priestly sacrifice on earth at the cross rather than in heaven.

Similarly, if the author has in mind an actual structure in heaven, then the need for Moses to cleanse it seems odd (9:23)—why would something in the highest heaven need to be cleansed? Indeed, the author explicitly makes a metaphor out of the sanctuary when he compares Christ's flesh to the tabernacle's veil (10:20).[21] At another point he seems to say that Christ entered the heavenly sanctuary by means of the heavenly sanctuary—a redundant statement if a literal structure is in view (9:11–12). Did God show Moses an exact blueprint for the *two*-room wilderness tabernacle (8:5)? At least after Christ's "sacrifice" the author's theology has no place for an outer room in the heavenly sanctuary: Christ's heaven has no room for barriers that partition off God's presence from his people (9:8).

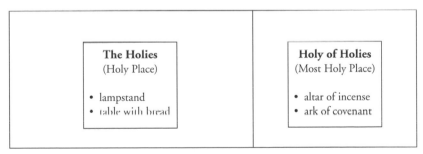

The Holies (Holy Place) • lampstand • table with bread	Holy of Holies (Most Holy Place) • altar of incense • ark of covenant

Figure 7

The reason these images break down is because they are primarily metaphorical in nature rather than literal. The author does not think of a literal structure in heaven or that Christ literally carried physical blood into the heavenly realm. Rather, these images are a part of his high priestly metaphor. The heavenly Holy of Holies is not a structure in heaven, but heaven itself metaphorically conceived (9:24). Christ's entrance into this Most Holy Place is thus the same event as his exaltation to God's right hand. When Hebrews uses traditional Christian imagery, Christ's sacrifice is offered on the cross. When the author is arguing from his high priestly metaphor, it is offered in heaven.

Christ's Sacrifice

A crucifixion was designed not only to kill people in a painful way but also to expose them to public ridicule as they died. Romans hoisted up such persons so that they were visible to all. In this light, to consider Christ's death as a sacrifice is a metaphor—crucifixion was literally a method of capital punishment filled with shame and disgrace. When Paul compared Christ's death to a sin offering, to the Passover lamb, or to the sacrifice made on the Day of Atonement, he was speaking metaphorically.[22] These images are all metaphors because they create new meaning by comparing two dissimilar things (e.g., a man to a lamb).

This basic metaphor in which Christ's death on the cross is a sacrifice for our sins underlies the more extended high priestly metaphor of Hebrews. For example, Heb. 9:27–28 seems to equate Christ's offering *with his death*. Hebrews 10:5, 10 indicate that it was Christ's *body* that was sacrificed. Indeed, the author's contrast between the earthly and the heavenly makes it highly unlikely that he thought earthly blood could or should be brought into the heavenly realm. On the contrary, Heb. 9:14 seems to say that it was "through eternal spirit" that Christ offered himself blameless to God in heaven.[23]

However, when the author is arguing from his high priestly metaphor, Christ becomes a Melchizedekian priest *in a heavenly sanctuary*. Hebrews 8:4 notes that "if he were on earth he would not be a priest, since there are [already] those who offer gifts [on earth] according to the law." Moreover, Christ is a minister "of the Most Holy Place and the true tent that the Lord pitched, not a man" (v. 2). Christ thus contrasts with the earthly priests of the earthly sanctuary. Herein is the tension: the traditional metaphor equated Christ's sacrifice with his death *on earth*; Hebrews's argument places the offering *in heaven*.

The key to understanding Hebrews's argument is to realize that the essence of all these sacrificial metaphors is the definitive means of reconciliation with God that Christ has provided in relation to our sins. Christ's death was an essential element in bringing about this atonement. But the comparison of Christ's victorious passage through the heavens to the entrance of the high priest into the Holy of Holies is an equally if not more potent picture of atonement. We do not have to harmonize the two images together to appreciate their meaning.

In keeping with the metaphorical nature of Christ's sacrifice, the author implicitly compares it to a number of different sacrificial moments in the Pentateuch. Of course, the primary contrast is with the sacrifice the high priest offered on the Day of Atonement. While priests performed their duties all year round in the outer room of the tent (e.g., 9:6), only *once* a year did the high priest enter the Most Holy Place, or as Heb. 9 refers to it, the "second tent."[24] Similarly, Christ entered *once* for all time into heaven itself, fully accomplishing our salvation (v. 26).

However, Hebrews also alludes to several other instances of atonement and cleansing in the law, contrasting them with the singular sacrifice of Christ as well. Hebrews 9:13 contrasts Christ's blood not only to the blood of bulls and goats, such as was offered on the Day of Atonement, but also to the ashes of a red heifer that were used in the ritual cleansing of those who came into contact with dead bodies (Num. 19:9, 17–19). Hebrews 9:19 contrasts Christ's offering not only with Moses' inauguration of the wilderness tent (Exod. 24:3, 6–8) but also with the red thread and hyssop that were used to cleanse those with infectious skin diseases (Lev. 14:4; also used in the red heifer ceremony, Num. 19:6). In short, Christ's onetime sacrifice is the corresponding equivalent to *all* the sacrifices of the old covenant, definitively replacing them all.

In the high priestly metaphor, what makes Christ's sacrifice effective over and against these old covenant sacrifices is the fact that it is a heavenly rather than an earthly one. The gifts and sacrifices of the old covenant, for example, were "require-ments of *flesh* enacted on the basis of foods, drinks, and various washings until the time of reformation" (Heb. 9:10). They were thus never able to cleanse the wor-shipers in terms of their *conscience* (v. 9).[25] The ashes of a heifer may have sancti-fied the unclean person's *flesh* (v. 13), but they did not actually take away sins (10:4).

On the other hand, what Christ has offered is not a matter of flesh or the "handmade" sanctuary. He makes his offering in heaven itself (8:3, 4; 9:24). He does not carry literal blood into heaven but "offered himself blameless to God through eternal spirit" (9:14). If his blood on the cross contrasts with the blood of bulls and goats on earth, then the *flesh* offered in the earthly sanctuary con-trasts with the *spirit* Christ offers in heaven itself.

The author can and does refer to *the* Holy Spirit when he is referring to Scrip-ture and revelation (e.g., 3:7; 9:8; 10:15), evoking strong images of God's per-son. He can also speak of holy spirit in a less personal way that implies participation in the substance of the divine realm (e.g., 2:4; 6:4). Finally, he can refer to the human spirit as that aspect of a person that pertains to the heavenly realm (e.g., 4:12; 12:9, 23).

When Heb. 9:14 says that Christ offered himself to God "through eternal spirit," many scholars think it means through *the Holy Spirit*, which is certainly possible grammatically even though the word *the* does not appear in the Greek text. Yet in Hebrews, the absence of the word *the* usually points to a different nuance for the word *spirit*.[26] Given the fact that the "indestructible life" of Christ (7:16), his "permanent priesthood" (v. 24), and the fact that he "always lives to intercede to God" are so important for the author (in fact the essence of his Melchizedekian priesthood), a reference to *Christ's* eternal spirit is the most appropriate interpretation of the verse. The fact that it is the *spirits* of the per-fected righteous that reach heaven (12:23) where the father of *spirits* is (v. 9) leads us to believe that 9:14 refers to Christ's liberated spirit ascending to heaven more than to the Holy Spirit (cf. 13:20).[27]

Christ's blood on the cross provides an effective sacrifice for sins because it is innocent blood. Christ is able to defeat the power of the devil as a blameless sac-rifice that atones, just as the blood of the Maccabean martyrs was thought to bring an end to God's wrath on Israel in a previous generation (cf. 2 Macc. 7:38). With the metaphor of Christ's heavenly high priesthood, however, the author can pit Christ against *all* the sacrifices of the old covenant. He offers a definitive sacrifice of blameless spirit in contrast to the perpetual earthly sacrifices of flesh. As such, his sacrifice is actually able to cleanse the conscience and take away sins, unlike all the fleshly sacrifices of the old covenant.

The Heavenly Sanctuary

The nature of the heavenly sanctuary in Hebrews stands at the center of the debate over the background of the epistle's thought.[28] For those who think the author was a Platonist, the heavenly tent is the Platonic pattern of which the earthly tabernacle was a copy.[29] For those who read Hebrews in terms of Jewish apocalyptic literature, the heavenly tabernacle is the heavenly temple of 2 Bar. 4 or the *Songs of Sabbath Sacrifice* from the Dead Sea Scrolls. For others it is the cosmological sanctuary of Philo and Josephus or a metaphor for something else like the body of Christ. Each interpretation has its favorite verses and in many instances can make a plausible case.

Hebrews 8:5 is the key verse for those who interpret the sanctuary in Platonic terms.[30] According to some translations, this verse speaks of the earthly sanctuary as a "shadow and copy" of the heavenly one, language that Hebrews repeats in 9:23 and 10:1. For Plato, things in the physical world are only shadows and copies of the true realities in the unchanging world of patterns and forms. When God tells Moses to construct the wilderness tent after the "type shown you on the mountain," the Platonic interpretation understands this "type" to be a Platonic pattern.

In chapter 2 we saw that Hebrews may indeed have Middle Platonic elements to its thought, chiefly in terms of its heaven/earth and flesh/spirit dualism. Nevertheless, a number of significant differences make a *purely* Platonic interpretation highly unlikely. For one thing, if the author meant to use Platonic language, he did not do a very good job of it. While the word for "shadow" in Heb. 8:5 is the same as that used in Platonic writings, the word sometimes translated "copy" rarely if ever means anything like this.[31] It more often than not means an "example" (cf. 4:11 where the same word is used) and is never directly used by any Platonist to describe the pattern/copy relationship.

Similarly, if the author wished to get a Platonic interpretation across, he would no doubt have used Exod. 25:9 rather than 25:40 to say that God showed Moses how to build the tabernacle. The former verse actually uses the key Platonic term *paradeigma* or "pattern." Instead Hebrews quoted the latter verse, which used the word *type*—a word that *can* have a Platonic meaning but less clearly so.[32]

Further, while the notion that the earthly *sanctuary* is a shadowy copy of a Platonic pattern sounds somewhat plausible by itself, it is more difficult to imagine how *events* could take place in a Platonic pattern. And the events that define the heavenly sanctuary occur long after the events of the so-called "copy." The contrast between the two sanctuaries is as much a past/present contrast as it is an earthly/heavenly one.

In the author's high priestly metaphor, it is important that Christ *enter* into the heavenly sanctuary—again a strange notion if the heavenly tent is some kind of Platonic pattern. Hebrews 9:24 states that unlike the handmade "holies" into which the earthly high priest entered, Christ entered into "heaven itself, now to appear before the face of God on our behalf."[33] This entrance is equivalent to Christ's exaltation to God's right hand. Hebrews 8:1–2 states similarly that "we have such a great high priest who sat at the right hand of the throne of majesty in the heavens, a minister of the 'holies' and the true tent." In this latter respect, the heavenly temple of Jewish apocalyptic literature has one advantage over the Platonic model—it can support a movement through space such as Christ makes during his exaltation. Hebrews 8:5 might make us think of a literal two-chamber structure in heaven of which the earthly tabernacle of Moses was a mirror image.

Yet the apocalyptic interpretation also faces a number of problems, such as the fact that Hebrews does not clearly refer to a *two-part* structure in heaven. Hebrews 9:24, cited in the preceding paragraph, makes the earthly Holy of Holies correspond to heaven itself, not to one room of a building in heaven.[34] In fact, Heb. 9:8–9 indicate that the outer room of the sanctuary symbolized the ineffectiveness of the earthly sanctuary as a whole. The fact that the high priest could enter the Holy of Holies only once a year symbolized the need to remove the "first tent" so that access to the "second tent" could be gained. The author says that this is a parable of the current situation in which earthly sacrifices simply do not remove sin. With the removal of the first tent, access to the second will occur. The author thus attaches a negative connotation to the outer room of the sanctuary such that it is hard to imagine the heavenly sanctuary having one.[35]

It is all too tempting to see a connection between the removal of the outer room of the sanctuary and the removal of the created realm in Heb. 12:27. In fact, we would argue that the high priestly metaphor is basically built off an understanding of the universe as the sanctuary of God—a "cosmological" temple.[36] The highest heaven itself is the heavenly sanctuary and Holy of Holies, where God's throne of grace is located. The heavenly sanctuary of Christ could have no outer room, however, just as the heavenly city of Revelation has no temple, "for the Lord God Almighty is its temple, and the Lamb" (Rev. 21:22). Here is an explanation for why the author makes such a sharp distinction between the outer and inner rooms of the sanctuary—it coheres with his sharp distinction between the created realm and the heaven where God dwells. Some scholars have in fact equated the outer room of the heavenly tabernacle with the created skies/heavens that lay below the highest heaven.[37] After all, Christ passed through these heavens (Heb. 4:14) on his way to a final destination even higher than they (7:26).

Yet even the cosmological temple must yield to the metaphorical nature of the author's argument. What is important for him is that God's heaven be thought of as a heavenly sanctuary, particularly as the heavenly Holy of Holies into which Christ entered when he sat at God's right hand. One of the clearest instances where

> **chiasm** A literary device that functions on an A B B' A' pattern. The first and last lines correspond to each other, as do the B and B' lines. It is possible to have an infinite number of other corresponding lines (e.g., C and C').

all literal interpretations of the heavenly tent break down is in Heb. 9:11. This verse is structured chiastically; that is, it has an A B B' A' pattern where the first and last statements are parallel, as are the second and third:

"Christ, having arrived as a high priest of good things accomplished,

A *through* the greater and more perfect tent,
B *not* handmade (that is not of this creation),
B' *nor* through the blood of bulls and goats, but
A' *through* his own blood,

entered once and for all into the 'holies.'"

The parallelism between line A and line A' indicates that the preposition "through" should be taken in both cases as the *means through* which Christ entered into the heavenly "holies" (not as a space *through* which he passed). Yet this interpretation results in the almost redundant claim that by means of the greater and more perfect tent, Christ entered the heavenly Holy of Holies. The key to appreciating this statement is to realize that the author does not have a literal structure in view. One must step back from its detail and see the way in which its various parts state the superiority of heaven to earth and the victory over sin that is entailed in Christ's passage through heaven.

Realizing the ultimately metaphorical nature of the heavenly tent gets us out of some other sticky interpretive problems. For example, scholars have often puzzled over the fact that the heavenly sanctuary needs cleansing in Heb. 9:23. Some have tried to alleviate the discomfort of the image by noting that the author is referring to the *inauguration* of the heavenly tabernacle, but the reason the wilderness tabernacle needed cleansing at its inauguration was because of the sinful hands that built it. Since God pitched the heavenly tent (8:2), such a cleansing would not seem necessary.

The key once again is to realize that the author is not picturing an actual structure in heaven nor does he think Christ carried literal blood into heaven. The extended metaphor of Christ's high priesthood is about the fact that he has victoriously accomplished the possibility of salvation. The inauguration of the heavenly sanctuary is not an actual ceremony that ever took place but a way of speaking of Christ's atoning death that inaugurated the possibility of atonement. It is the sins of those who come to God through Christ's sacrifice that are really cleansed, not some building in heaven.

CONCLUSION

Going beyond anything that appears elsewhere in the pages of the New Testament, the Epistle to the Hebrews argues from a sweeping metaphor that pits

Christ against the entirety of the Old Testament sacrificial system. When Christ comes as a priest from the order of Melchizedek, he signals a change in priesthood, the end of the Levitical order. Levitical priests first had to make atonement for their own sins before they sacrificed for the people. They also died regularly and thus could not maintain their priestly duties indefinitely. In the order of Melchizedek, Christ remains a priest forever and has no sins of his own for which to atone.

Corresponding to the various types of sacrifices in the Old Testament, none of which actually took away sin, Christ's death and subsequent entrance into heaven constitutes an effective offering that is once and for all. Unlike those who enter into handmade sanctuaries, Christ entered into heaven itself. The author thus compares Christ's exaltation at God's right hand to his entrance into a heavenly sanctuary, a metaphor for the atonement God has now made available through Christ. Because of him we can now approach God with boldness (Heb. 4:16; 10:19).

We must suppose that the metaphor of Christ's high priesthood carried a certain force when it played itself out in the author's recurring exhortations for the audience to hold fast their confession. He is not just giving interesting ideas about Christ; he is making a theoretical argument that he believes will impact the audience's current situation. The next chapter will explore what that impact might have been.

Chapter 6

The Situation of the Audience

INTRODUCTION

Our travel through the story world of Hebrews has led us across time and space. We have seen heaven and earth, past and present. We have looked at various characters in the plot ranging from the superb Abel to the faithless Esau. We have joined in the celebration of the enthroned Christ as he offers the definitive solution to humanity's problem. We look forward to God's unshakable kingdom when the created realm is removed and the defeat of the devil complete.

However, what we have not looked at in great detail is the specific place of the audience of Hebrews in that overarching story. To be sure, we have picked up hints here and there about how they fit in the plot. We know that the various examples of belief and disbelief the author mentions relate directly to his desire for the audience to hold fast in their confession of hope (Heb. 10:23). We also know that the things he teaches relate to whatever is standing in the way of their continuance in faith. We have tried to keep in mind that Hebrews tells the story of salvation history for a reason—it is not a disinterested telling of the story. Rather, the author has presented the story the way he has in order to serve his rhetorical purposes.

Many studies on Hebrews begin with a discussion of the epistle's context and its great unknowns. They guess at the identity of the author and audience at the start. They present hypotheses about the point of origin and location to which it was written. Front-loading such questions runs the danger of biasing their interpretation in the direction of highly tendentious reconstructions. For this reason we left the question of the audience's situation till last so that our interpretation of the story and rhetoric of Hebrews could stand somewhat on its own before we began to hazard guesses about particulars.[1]

THE BACKGROUND OF THE AUDIENCE

A good method to follow on any matter of disagreement is to move from the agreed to the controversial, from the more certain to the unclear. We can infer a number of fairly uncontroversial things about Hebrews's audience before we get to matters of less agreement. For example, the Greek of Hebrews is perhaps the best in the New Testament, and its argument is based exclusively on a Greek translation of the Hebrew Scriptures. From this observation it becomes clear that both its author and audience were Greek speakers.[2] This fact significantly, but not decisively, increases the likelihood that Hebrews was written to a destination other than Jerusalem or the Jewish homeland.

The audience is "Christian."[3] They have figuratively left "Egypt" (Heb. 3:16). They have been baptized and have partaken of holy spirit (6.1–5). The blood of Christ has atoned for their sins and sanctified them (10:26–29). In short, they have fully undergone the process of normalization into the "people of God" as the author understands it.

They have been Christians for some time. During a time of earlier persecution, they had been exemplary models of faith (6:10; 10:32). They had endured disgrace by associating with Christians in prison and had given them assistance (10:33–34). They had even accepted the plundering of their property "with joy." After giving them a stern warning, the author affirms optimistically that God will remember them for the "work and love you have demonstrated in the name of [God] by the way you have served and still serve the saints" (6:10).

Hebrews 13:7 states further, "remember your leaders who spoke the word of God to you. As you consider the outcome of their way of life, imitate their faith." While not all agree, this statement most naturally implies that these former leaders have already died, probably by way of martyrdom. As we will see, a significant number of statements in Hebrews have overtones of hardship, persecution, and even martyrdom. Perhaps the author thinks the audience will soon suffer intensely for their faith as well—a fact that might also be an element in their wavering commitment.

The author and audience are second-generation Christians, and the author is not an apostle. The message of salvation he preaches was first spoken by the Lord and only later "was confirmed to us *by those who heard him*" (2:3). Even aside from the significant differences between Paul and Hebrews in terms of style, vocabulary, and thought, this comment in itself eliminates Paul as a possible author for Hebrews. The man who argued so vigorously that he had witnessed the risen Lord (e.g., 1 Cor. 9:1) would scarcely say he was dependent on some other witness for confirmation of the gospel (cf. Gal. 1:11–12).[4]

On the other hand, the author and audience of Hebrews were quite possibly acquainted or connected with the Pauline mission, and Paul may very well have been one of those whose faith the author tells the audience to imitate in Heb. 13:7. Not only does the author associate himself with a "Timothy" who has just been released from prison (13:23), but Hebrews shares a number of traditions in

Parallels Between Hebrews and Paul

1. The mention of a "Timothy" in Heb. 13:23

2. Common early Christian tradition
   - The use of Ps. 8 in conjunction with Ps. 110:1 (1 Cor. 15:25–27; Heb. 1:13; 2:6–8)
   - Similar apocalyptic features such as the enslavement of the creation to demonic powers (e.g., Rom. 8:19–22; Heb. 2:14)
   - The use of Hab. 2:4 (Rom. 1:17; Heb. 10:38, Paul uses *faith* more in the sense of trust, Hebrews in the sense of faithfulness)
   - Use of new covenant imagery from Jer. 31 (2 Cor. 3:6; Heb. 8:6, 8)
   - Christ's death as a sacrifice (Rom. 3:25; Heb. 2:17)
   - Christ as priest? (Rom. 8:34; Heb. 5, 7–10)

3. Both stand on the same side of the Jewish law issue (cf. new covenant language).
   - Paul does not require Gentiles to keep the law (=primarily boundary marker practices) and argues that both Jew and Gentile are justified on the basis of faith. *The law functioned in the interim before Christ.*
   - Hebrews argues that the Jewish Law (=primarily sacrificial system) was only a foreshadowing of what Christ would do. *The Law functioned in the period before Christ.*

4. Other common elements
   - Dualism of heaven/earth (e.g., Gal. 4:24–26, which uses heavenly/earthly Jerusalem imagery not completely unlike Heb. 12:18–24)
   - Dualism of spirit/flesh (e.g., Rom. 8:5; Heb. 9:14, Hebrews's contrast is more rational in overtone, Paul's more apocalyptic)
   - Incongruity of sin in Christian practice (e.g., Rom. 6:1–2; Gal. 5:16; Heb. 10:26)
   - The primacy of grace in salvation (e.g., Gal. 2:21; Heb. 10:29)
   - Athletic imagery (e.g., 1 Cor. 9:24–27; Heb. 5:14; 12:1)
   - Infancy/maturity language (1 Cor. 3:2; Heb. 5:12–14; cf. 1 Pet. 2:2)
   - Expository material preceding exhortation section (e.g., Rom. 1–11/12–16; Heb. 1–10/10–13)

5. Similarities to other writings with Pauline elements
   - 1 Peter—"people of God" (1 Pet. 2:10; Heb. 4:9); context of suffering (1 Pet. 1:6; 2:21; 4:12; Heb. 12:2–4); exile imagery (1 Pet. 1:1, 17; 2:11; Heb. 11:13); use of Ps. 110:1 and apocalyptic imagery (1 Pet. 3:22; 5:8; Heb. 1:13; 2:14); use of priestly and sacrificial imagery (1 Pet. 1:19; 2:5, 9; Heb. 7–10; 13:15); necessity for holiness (1 Pet. 1:15–16; Heb. 12:14); Christ as Shepherd (1 Pet. 2:25; Heb. 13:20); importance of hospitality (1 Pet. 4:9; Heb. 13:2); do not be greedy (1 Pet. 5:2; Heb. 13:5)
   - Colossians—Middle Platonic christological imagery, including Christ as agent of creation (Col. 1:15–16; Heb. 1:2–3); use of Ps. 110:1 (Col. 3:1; Heb. 1:13); apocalyptic imagery, including Christ in contrast to angels (Col. 1:16; 2:15, 18; Heb. 1; 2:14); cancellation of the Jewish law (Col. 2:14; Heb. 7:18); strange law-related teaching aimed at Gentiles (Col. 2:16, 21; Heb. 13:9); law a shadow (Col. 2:17; Heb. 10:1)

Figure 8

common with Paul's writings (see Fig. 8). It is probably no coincidence that Hebrews also has similarities to Colossians and 1 Peter, two other books often connected with the Pauline circle.[5]

It seems likely that Rome (or Italy) is either the destination or point of origin for the epistle. A good number of scholars have opted for a Roman destination, a destination we consider most likely as well in the light of 13:24.[6] The default sense of the word *from* used in this verse is that of separation "away from" rather than source "from," making "those *away from* Italy" the most natural sense of the phrase. Surely it is also significant that the earliest references to Hebrews come from Clement *of Rome* in the 90s of the Common Era.[7] At times Clement's allusions to material from the epistle are quite thick. While a copy of a significant letter was often kept at its point of origin, Clement's frequent allusions to Hebrews more likely reflect the reverberations of a sermon sent in the recent past to the churches of Rome.[8]

The greatest objection to a Roman destination is the author's statement in Heb. 12:4 that the audience has "not yet resisted to the point of blood as you struggle against sin." A number of Roman Christians did lose their lives in the Neronian persecution.[9] If that crisis was the one in which previous leaders of the community passed from the scene (13:7), then a Roman audience for the epistle would indeed have resisted "to the point of blood" in the past. Many interpreters find this objection significant enough to opt for a different destination or at least to date the epistle prior to the bulk of Nero's persecution.[10] Given that Jewish Christians at Rome probably did lose property during the reign of Claudius (41–54 C.E.; cf. Heb. 10:34), some scholars place Hebrews at the beginning of Nero's persecution of the church.[11]

On the other hand, perhaps the author has a specific "struggle against sin" in mind, one that has newly cropped up in the community. If so, then the comment would only mean that the current crisis they face has not yet escalated to the point of martyrdom. Still others suggest that Hebrews was directed at a specific house church or Christian synagogue in Rome that had not lost any to the Neronian persecution. It is sometimes pointed out that one of the thirteen synagogues we know of in Rome around this time was called the Synagogue *of the Hebrews*.[12]

A more important issue for interpretation is the ethnic makeup of the audience—whether they are Jewish Christians, Gentile Christians, or a mixed audience. This question has significant implications for what one thinks the immediate situation behind the epistle is. On the one hand, the majority of scholars have understandably concluded that the audience was Jewish Christian. One of the oldest suggestions about the situation of the audience is that they are Jewish Christians tempted to return to their pre-Christian beliefs and practices because of persecution or the delay of Christ's return. The author writes them of the superiority of the new covenant over the old so they will not return to mainstream Judaism.

This conclusion is understandable since the author argues so extensively from the details of the Old Testament. One might suggest that a Gentile audience would not have found arguments from the Old Testament persuasive if they doubted the truth of Christianity in the first place. And given how difficult it is for us to follow the argument at times, some question whether Gentile converts would have been able to understand the epistle in the first place. The author's exposition seems to target reliance on Levitical means of atonement, and the recurring contrasts of the epistle all target the Jewish law in one way or another. It is easier for us to see the relevance of such a sustained argument to Jewish rather than Gentile Christians. It is difficult for us to imagine how a Gentile would be drawn to the Levitical system in some way as a means of atonement.

On the other hand, none of these arguments decisively preclude a Gentile Christian audience, and they certainly do not indicate an exclusively Jewish one. For instance, the letters of Galatians and Colossians were both sent to Gentile audiences who were keeping the Jewish law in one way or another. This fact probably indicates that "conservative" forms of Jewish Christianity often had significant success in convincing Gentile converts to follow aspects of the Jewish law.

Even in the second century the church father Ignatius could write to the Gentiles of Magnesia "if we are living according to Judaism until now, we confess that we have not received grace." His comments indicate that observance of the Jewish law by Gentiles continued in Asia Minor into the second century. Further, books like Galatians and 1 Peter, even though they are written to Gentiles, still expect their audiences to be able to follow arguments drawn from the Old Testament. Just as Gentile Christians today usually consider the Old Testament to be their "property," the Old Testament became Scripture to ancient Gentile converts to Christianity as well.[13]

> If someone interprets Judaism to you, do not hear them. It is better to hear Christianity from someone who is circumcised than to learn Judiasm from someone uncircumcised.
>
> —Ign. *Phld.* 6.1

This latter observation raises the question of whether the argument of Heb. 2:16 addresses its audience as *ethnic* sons of Abraham or as *"adopted"* sons of Abraham. The argument of Heb. 2 implies that the author has already redefined the idea of the "seed of Abraham" to include Gentiles. The author understands Ps. 8 to be about *all* humanity, and Christ tastes death *on behalf of all* (Heb. 2:9). So when Heb. 2:16 notes that the "seed of Abraham" are Christ's concern, it clearly incorporates Gentiles into its understanding of what true Israel is. Old Testament imagery becomes the "property" of Jewish and Gentile Christians equally without distinction.

It is therefore no coincidence that the words *Jew* and *Gentile* do not appear in Hebrews. The author refers to the "people of God" rather than to ethnic Israel or the Jews (e.g., 2:17; 4:9; 11:25).[14] These features would make sense if a significant portion of its audience were Gentile. Interestingly, while Paul's letter to the Romans (ca. 58 C.E.) seems to address an audience of mixed ethnicity, the Roman church on balance at that time appears to be more Gentile than Jewish (e.g., Rom. 1:13; 6:19; 10:1–2). A number of scholars have argued that while the church at Rome remained primarily Gentile in the years that followed, it nonetheless had a strong affinity with the relatively "conservative" Jewish Christianity of Peter and James.[15]

It is also interesting that the list of basic instructions the audience needs to relearn is not specifically "Christian": The list looks like the kinds of things a convert *to Judaism* would need to learn, not a Jew who had joined the Christian movement. Why would a Jew need to learn what "faith in God" or "the resurrection of the dead" meant (Heb. 6:1–2)? David deSilva has recently made a case that the phrase "dead works" in Heb. 6:1 evokes the image of idol worship, scarcely something for which a Jew would usually need to repent.[16] In short, the catechetical list of Heb. 6:1–2 would more naturally apply to a Gentile convert to Christianity than to a Jew who found in Christ the fulfillment of God's promises to Israel. We should thus probably think the audience to be of mixed ethnicity, with a predominantly Gentile makeup.

> Miserable are also their hopes in *dead things*, who have called the works of human hands "gods," gold and silver, skillful work.
> —Wis. 13:10

THE EPISTLE'S EXHORTATIONS AND THE SITUATION

Chapter 4 looked at how the author of Hebrews used various characters from the plot of salvation history to motivate his audience to action. The wilderness generation and Esau were negative examples that the author wished the audience to shun while Heb. 11 presented a cloud of witnesses to emulate. From these exhortations we can infer a number of things about how the author at least perceived the situation of the audience.

First of all, the belief that Christ was at least potentially about to return to earth stands in the background of the author's exhortations. The author believed that Christ would soon save those awaiting him (9:28; 10:35–39), and the final judgment would begin. Both positively and negatively, the author's exhortations encourage the audience to maintain their "confession of hope" until that day (10:23), the day when they would definitively enter God's rest and cease from their earthly labors as God did on the seventh day (4:9–10). Like the wilderness generation, they face the question of whether they will continue to be faithful to God's promise or whether they will fall in the desert (3:16–19). Like Esau, they potentially could throw away their sonship for something earthly and trivial (12:16).

Scholars disagree over how real these threats were. Some think the author was primarily reinforcing values the audience was not really in danger of abandoning. Others think overtones of hardship are more a rhetorical device than a response to a real situation. Yet the author gives us ample reason to think he is responding to real circumstances in the lives of his audience. Even if he believes they will make the right decisions in the end, the danger of leaving the people of God seems to be real.

For example, the author indicates that some in the community have stopped attending the Christian assembly (10:25). He refers to their "drooping hands and weakened knees" (12:12), and Hebrews is the only New Testament letter to threaten its audience with a permanent loss of salvation (6:4–8; 10:26–31; 12:16–17). In our opinion, the chiding of verses like 5:11–6:12 is too strong not to be in response to something the author perceives as a real crisis in the community. He calls the audience "dull of hearing" (5:11; 6:12), "infants" (5:13), and in 12:8 suggests they will be illegitimate sons if they do not submit to God's discipline.

The comparison of the audience's situation to a father's "discipline" indicates that more is going on than just a waning of confidence in the Christian message. Some have suggested that the author wrote the epistle to bolster the audience's confidence in Christianity given a delay in Christ's return. Such doubt may indeed be an element in the equation (cf. 10:35–39), but it is not the only element. In the mind of the author, and probably in the mind of the audience, the recipients of Hebrews face potential hardship and persecution. The author thinks God is currently disciplining them as a father disciplines his sons (12:5–11).

Such "discipline" need not refer primarily to punishment, although the author probably sees an element of this kind of discipline in the audience's circumstances. Discipline can also refer to training. Accordingly, the author believes that the current "training" the audience is undergoing will "repay righteousness" and produce a "peaceful fruit" (12:11). He is hoping that they, like Jesus, will "learn obedience through the things that they suffer" (5:8).

A number of the exhortations in Hebrews hint that the author thinks the audience is facing or may soon face persecution. For example, the witnesses of Heb. 11:35b–38 did not escape suffering even though they were faithful. They are those who were stoned, sawed in half, tortured, flogged, put in prison, exiled to deserts, caves, and mountains. While the author begins this section of Heb. 11 with those who were victorious in faith (vv. 32–35a), he *climaxes* the list of witnesses with those who accepted defeat in the earthly realm. It is these witnesses in particular that lead into the author's exhortation in verses 12:1–2 to continue running the race of faithfulness with patience. Such imagery would be highly appropriate if the possibility of persecution were on the minds of the audience.

The epistle/sermon also includes a number of allusions to the hope of resurrection, a hope that would again be especially pertinent if the possibility of martyrdom were in the minds of the audience. For example, the author may very well allude to the martyrs of 2 Macc. 7 when he mentions those who "did not receive redemption so they could obtain a better resurrection" (Heb. 11:35). The author's descriptions of several other witnesses to faith in the early part of Heb. 11 also have overtones of resurrection. Although in a sense the descendents of Abraham were "dead" because he was too old to have children, God brought them to life by the miraculous birth of Isaac (v. 12). In a figure, Abraham received Isaac back *from the dead* when God prevented his sacrifice. Indeed, Abraham offered him in the first place because he had faith that God could raise *the dead*

(v. 19). Jacob and Joseph both look forward to the future of Israel well beyond their deaths (vv. 21–22). In short, a number of the examples in Heb. 11 seem calculated to bolster the audience's faith in their continued existence beyond death and the certainty of God's promises about the future.

The cumulative effect of such rhetoric is the impression that potential hardship and suffering as Christians is a factor in the waning commitment of some in the audience to Christ. Indeed, the greatest example of endurance the author gives is that of Christ. We have already mentioned the author's carefully worded observation that Jesus "learned obedience through the things that he suffered, even though he was a son" (5:8). In the light of Heb. 12, the author surely worded this statement this way as an implicit exhortation to the audience to endure the suffering they face.

Christ is a high priest who can sympathize with the weaknesses of the audience since he was tempted (to escape death?) as they are, yet did not sin in the course of his temptation (2:18; 4:15). He came in the first place to free them from the fear and slavery of death (2:15). He was a model for the one who faces death as a consequence of faithfulness to God, offering "petitions and supplications with strong crying and tears" as he faced death. Because of his godly fear God saved him out of death in answer to his prayers (5:7). More than any of the other witnesses to faith, it is to his example most of all that the audience is to look—this one "who for the joy that was set before him endured the cross, having despised the shame" (12:2). The audience is to consider "the one who endured such opposition from sinners against him" (v. 3). These comments indicate strongly that the audience is in a situation with a foreboding air to it, one in which "sinners" of some sort pose at least the threat of persecution and perhaps even martyrdom.

Therefore, it is not unreasonable to suggest that the "sin" and "sinners" of Heb. 12:4 are a specific threat in the life of the community. Accordingly, this verse need not eliminate Rome as a destination or preclude a date after the Neronian persecution. The verse simply indicates that the audience has not yet faced martyrdom in their current situation. We may be able to glean clues about the nature of this external pressure from the way the author has crafted some of the other examples in Heb. 11.

On the one hand, Jewish opposition would not likely present the threat of martyrdom—although it could serve as a catalyst for martyrdom.[17] If the audience potentially faces death, the actual killer is most likely the ruling authorities of their locale. Interestingly, several aspects of the author's description of Moses carry overtones of persecution by a ruler. These overtones would play well into the suggestion of Rome as the epistle's destination, with Christians fearing the potential of persecution by the emperor.

In Heb. 11:23, Moses' parents demonstrate faith by disobeying the *edict of the king* without fear. Moses chooses to suffer with the people of God rather than to enjoy the pleasures of *sin* for a brief period. He chooses to receive shame rather than to enjoy the treasures of "Egypt" (vv. 24–25). These images would have great significance to Roman citizens potentially faced with the choice of Caesar or Christ.

Indeed, Heb. 11:27 is somewhat enigmatic in the way it uses Moses' departure from Egypt as an example of his *lack* of fear of the king's anger. If his flight from Egypt after killing an Egyptian is in view, Moses fled on that occasion because he *was* afraid. On the other hand, if the author is evoking the image of exile, the verse could represent a willingness to face exile out of faithfulness to Christ over and against the king. In all these statements, it is tempting to see Egypt and Jericho as allusions to Rome (vv. 29–30), with "the king" of these verses being a not-so-subtle reference to the Roman emperor.

If this interpretation were correct, the two main candidates would be Nero and Domitian. Of these two, a persecution of Christians is well attested during the reign of Nero, who likely put Peter and Paul to death.[18] A somewhat popular suggestion for the occasion of Hebrews sees the epistle as a sermon to primarily Jewish Christians at Rome in the early 60s before Nero's persecution of the church became severe.

With regard to Domitian, many scholars now doubt whether Christians experienced significant persecution during his reign, although such a persecution was once a consensus among scholars.[19] However, what is important for Hebrews is not so much that an extensive persecution *actually* took place during his reign as that the circumstances were such that the author of Hebrews might have anticipated one. On the whole, we have good reason to believe that Christians experienced some hardship during the reign of Domitian and that many would have feared an escalation involving martyrdom. With the memory of what had happened during Nero's reign in the 60s, it is likely that Domitian's reign brought similar fears to the Christians at Rome.

Domitian's reign brought hardships for many in Rome, many of a financial nature. His assassination in 96 C.E. underlines this fact. For example, the Roman historian Cassius Dio tells us that Domitian had one of the highest ranking Roman officials put to death for "atheism" and taking on "Jewish ways."[20] He similarly sent this man's wife into exile, along with another man named Glabrio whom Domitian eventually put to death. While we cannot be certain that these individuals were Christians,[21] their deaths and banishment indicate an environment that could easily have produced a fear of martyrdom. After all, the Romans often considered Christians atheists because they did not participate in the state religion as well as in other cults.

> In the same year Domitian put to death many others, including Flavius Clemens who was consul, even though he was a cousin and had Flavia Domitilla as his wife—herself also a relative. And the charge of atheism was brought upon both, a charge on which also many others were condemned for running aground into the customs of the Jews. Some died, others were at least deprived of their possessions. Domitilla was only banished to Pandateria.
> —Cassius Dio, *Roman History* 67.14.1–2

Domitian is well known for his desire to be addressed as "Lord and God," an indulgence that no doubt put him at serious odds with both Jew and Christian.[22] A majority of scholars probably still see these attitudes as the basis for some of the imagery in Revelation,[23] and a number of early Christian writers indicated at least a limited persecution during his reign.[24] Finally, *1 Clem.* 1:1's reference to "the unforeseen and continuous misfortunes and terrors" that have recently come on the community at Rome has often been read in reference to hardships during Domitian's last years as emperor.

> With equal arrogance, when [Domitian] would issue a formal letter in the name of his procurators, he began them in this way, "Our Lord and God commands this to be done." From this point on it became customary that he not be addressed in any other way other than this way in writing or in conversation.
>
> —Suetonius, *Domitian* 13

Hebrews at more than one point encourages its audience to orient itself around its heavenly destination. Thus the patriarchs were looking for a "city" whose builder and maker is God (Heb. 11:10). They were not concerned with the "homeland" from which they departed; they looked for the heavenly one to come (11:14–16; cf. 2:5). The author urged his audience to go outside the camp and bear the shame of Christ, "for we do not have a city here that remains—we are seeking the one to come" (13:13–14).

This repeated imagery is so consistent and so clearly aimed as an exhortation to the audience that a real city/homeland is most likely in view. On the one hand, Jerusalem is a tempting suggestion. If the audience includes individuals tempted to rely on Levitical means of atonement, Jerusalem could be the city the author is urging them to leave behind. In such a case, the statement that we do not have a city down here on earth *that remains* could be meant in part to console Jewish Christians over the destruction of Jerusalem, a city that no longer "has foundations" (cf. 11:10).

However, if the persecution of Romans citizens who are also Christians is in view, then the city could also be Rome. While it is difficult for us to identify with the way many upper-class Romans viewed exile, the literature indicates that to some it was a fate almost worse than death.[25] Leaving the camp to bear Christ's reproach (13:13), not returning to the homeland from which they have departed (11:14), being strangers and aliens on the earth (v. 13)—these images could pertain to Gentile Christians who fear exile if they do not conform to the "edict of the king."[26]

We can imagine several ways in which Christians might have come into conflict with Roman law under the reign of Domitian. These include such charges as unlawful assembly, failure to pay the tax Domitian expected of the Jews,[27] or perhaps failure to participate in the state religion. In this last case, the author's mention of repentance "from dead works" (6:1) would take on special significance. If the author thought Domitian might require Christians to offer sacrifices to the gods, we would understand better why the issue of "second repentance" shows up so strongly in Hebrews.[28]

The first parable of the Shepherd of Hermas may recollect this period of the

Roman church when it alludes to the possibility of opposition from the emperor in language highly reminiscent of Hebrews. Hermas claims that the true country of the Christian is far from Rome: "the servants of God dwell in a strange [country], for your city is far from this city." He dissuades his audience from accumulating buildings, land, and property in Rome, for "the lord of this city will say, 'I do not want you to live in my city. Go out of this city because you do not use my law'" (Herm. *Sim.* 1.1–3). These words from second-century Rome provide strong evidence that the loss of property and land was a real possibility in the minds of Roman Christians, a memory from the past.

Since Domitian reigned from 81 to 96 C.E., this hypothesis would date Hebrews somewhere in the same general period as Revelation and not too long before *1 Clement.* The greatest objection to this dating is imagery that many take to imply that the Jerusalem temple was still operating at the time of writing. For example, the author uses the present tense in reference to the operation of the earthly sanctuary (e.g., Heb. 7:27–28; 8:3–5; 9:7 *and especially 9:9*; 9:25; 10:1; 13:11) and seems to imply that the old covenant with its continuous offering of sacrifices has not yet completely disappeared (8:13 and 10:2). Further, some think the author would surely have mentioned the destruction of the Jerusalem temple to bolster his case if he had written after 70 C.E.

However, none of these arguments are decisive against a post-70 C.E. date. Josephus, writing in the 90s, also refers to the operation of the Jewish temple in the present tense (e.g., *Ant.* 3.224–57; *Ag Ap.* 2.77, 193–8). More significant, so does Clement, who shows a recent acquaintance with Hebrews (*1 Clem.* 41:2). In short, while *we* know that the Jerusalem temple never resumed operation after 70 C.E. (and especially after the Bar Kokhba revolt of 132–35), both Jewish and Christian writers of the 90s give us no sense that *they* thought of the sacrificial system or even the Jerusalem temple in this way. The notion of Levitical atonement remained operative in theory well after the Jerusalem temple stood in ruin.

THE EPISTLE'S EXPOSITION AND THE SITUATION

If the *exhortations* of Hebrews give us reason to see the prospect of persecution from *Gentiles* as a major factor behind its writing, the *exposition* of Hebrews strangely points to reliance on the *Jewish* Levitical system as a reason. The argument of Hebrews presents Christ as the replacement of the Levitical system as a means of atonement. Therefore, when the author urges the audience to hold fast their confession of faith, one might naturally think the alternative in view was turning to the Jewish Levitical system in some way. The epistle thus gives us mixed signals with regard to its situation—while its argument pictures an audience relying on Jewish means of atonement, its exhortations picture an audience drifting away under the threat of Gentile persecution. It is no wonder so many different situations have been suggested for the epistle!

Starting once again with the more certain before moving to the more contested, we must affirm that Hebrews's argument does indeed have the Old Testament cultus in view. The cultic imagery of Hebrews is not a general polemic against pagan temples and sacrifices. While the author believes that the sacrifices of the Jewish tabernacle were clearly inferior, they were legitimate (Heb. 2:2) even if shadowy representations of the true, heavenly sanctuary (8:5; 10:1). While they could not cleanse the conscience, the author allows that they *did* effectively cleanse the flesh (9:13). On the other hand, it is inconceivable that the author would think a pagan temple or sacrifice could be effective in any way or even serve as a shadowy example of God's true sanctuary. The author views the Jewish cultus as inferior, not as evil.

Similarly, the author does not make reference to the Old Testament sacrificial system solely to show how great Christ is. On the one hand, it is true that a great deal of Hebrews's exposition is somewhat "theoretical" and does not explicitly target reliance on the Levitical cultus as an alternative to Christ's sacrifice. Thus, while the contrast between Christ and the angels is based on a contrast between the two covenants, Hebrews's *explicit* argument uses the contrast only as a basis for showing the greatness of Christ and the importance of being faithful to his message. The contrast of Christ and Moses in Heb. 3 and that between Christ and earthly high priests in Heb. 5 similarly seem very theoretical, calculated to bolster confidence in Christ rather than targeting an improper attitude toward the old covenant.

Yet the closer the argument gets to the Old Testament sacrificial system, the greater sense we get that the author thinks reliance on Levitical means of atonement poses a threat in some way to the community's continuance in faith. For example, it is the mention of Christ as a high priest after the order of Melchizedek that sets the author off on the most intense exhortation of the whole sermon. When the author resumes his discussion of Melchizedek in Heb. 7, he begins to argue pointedly for the first time that Christ's high priesthood is not only greater than that of the Levitical priests—it replaces their priesthood.

Up to this point the author had used elements from the old covenant primarily to emphasize the greatness of Christ and the importance of heeding his word. In Heb. 7–10, however, the author directly engages in an argument against reliance on the old covenant and its means of atonement. He argues extensively in Heb. 7 that Christ's high priesthood entails the discontinuation of the levitical priesthood (vv. 11–19). He calls the law "weak" and "useless" (v. 18). He indicates that the first covenant is on its way out (8:7–8, 13) and that Christ's sacrifice has definitively put an end to the Levitical sacrificial system (e.g., 10:9, 18).

Perhaps the strongest statement in this section is when he uses the imagery of the two-part sanctuary to argue that the way into the Most Holy Place is not possible while the earthly sacrificial system "has standing" (9:8). The implication is that reliance on Levitical means of atonement is not only unnecessary—it is a significant hindrance to proper access to God. In short, the author dedicates far too much of his argument to the superiority of Christ over the Levitical system for him not to think it poses a real threat to the audience's faith.

Those who focus on this aspect of the epistle understandably tend to favor a Jewish audience. They tend to think the audience is in danger of "shrinking back" into mainstream Judaism (10:39). Some think that the apostasy in question is a return to the Levitical system, thus denying the effectiveness of Christ's sacrifice (6:6). Some scholars connect the failing attendance at the Christian assembly (10:25) to a return to the synagogue. Some even suggest that the synagogue would have provided protection from persecution under the umbrella of Judaism's "legal" status. It is more difficult for us to see how Gentiles would be drawn to the Jewish sacrificial system in some way.

The clearest indication that reliance on the Levitical system is a live option for the audience comes from Heb. 13:9–10, also some of the most notoriously difficult verses in the epistle to interpret. Here the author says, "Do not be carried away by various strange teachings. It is good for the heart to be established by grace and not by foods—those who walked in them were not profited. We have an altar from which those who serve the tent do not have authority to eat." These verses, while they are not a focal point for the author's exhortations, nonetheless provide clues to the author's argument against reliance on the Old Testament cultus.

For example, a number of aspects to these verses parallel other statements in the author's previous argument. The mention of foods reminds us not only of Heb. 9:10, where the same word refers to elements of the sacrificial system in the wilderness tabernacle, but it also reminds us of how Esau gave his birthright away in exchange for food (12:16). The reference to the altar of the tabernacle in the following verse (13:10) confirms that such foods had a sacrificial meaning for some in the audience, and the mention of the tabernacle strongly evokes the argument of Heb. 9–10. These parallels suggest that some in the audience are relying or are tempted to rely in some way on "foods" that have sacrificial significance to them, foods that they connect in some way with Levitical atonement.

These foods are not likely literal sacrifices at the Jerusalem temple, although in the period before the destruction of the temple Diaspora Jews regularly took up collections so that sacrifices could be offered for them in Jerusalem.[29] However, Hebrews's argument circles entirely around the wilderness tabernacle—it is a theoretical argument that never so much as even mentions the temple. Of course, no one who served the actual tent had been living for well over a thousand years when Hebrews was written, but we cannot preclude the possibility that individuals of priestly lineage are involved in the "foods" mentioned in this passage. Presuming a Diaspora context for Hebrews, the most likely context for a meal thought to have atoning value based on the Levitical system would be some communal meal in a Jewish synagogue.[30] The author's exhortation to leave the "camp" and suffer "outside the gate" (13:11–12) could refer to shame resulting from alienation from one's peers in the synagogue. Such alienation might also involve the potential charge of illegal assembly. While Jews had a longstanding right to congregate, other groups needed express permission from the Romans (cf. Acts 19:20).

While the evidence becomes increasingly sketchy, these verses give us a clear basis for seeing an inappropriate connection (at least in the mind of the author) between some in Hebrews's audience and the Jewish synagogue. "Those who serve the tent" cannot be Christians since such individuals *would* have authority to eat from the Table of Christ. Moreover, the fact that reproach ensues on leaving the camp implies that real people are involved, not just a theoretical abandonment of outdated theology. We can see the attractiveness of the suggestion that the recipients were Jews in conflict with their identity and heritage.

It is at this point that the suggestion that the audience is primarily Gentile becomes most difficult. It is difficult for us to imagine what circumstances would draw Gentiles to Levitical means of atonement. We might wonder how persecution might make mainstream Judaism become attractive to such Gentiles. Would association with the Jewish synagogue provide protection from persecution by the Romans or from the charge of atheism? The kinds of hypotheses necessary to account for all the data become increasingly complex with only scanty evidence to support them.

Yet the fact that a Gentile hypothesis involves complexity does not necessarily mean it is on the wrong track. After all, we have come to this point because of our attempt to follow the most likely conclusions of each particular piece of evidence. The process has led us to the perimeter of our knowledge of Christianity and Judaism in late-first-century Rome. Yet perhaps the evidence is pointing in directions that will increase that knowledge and our understanding of the Christian writings of Rome from this period. We wonder if Roman Christianity of the late first century retained a strongly Jewish character. We wonder if the Gentile Christians of Rome had largely been "God-fearers" at some time prior to becoming Christians. We wonder if association with Roman synagogues might have provided some shield for Gentile Christians from Roman prosecution.

First of all, a good case can be made that much of Roman Christianity, while primarily Gentile, was strongly Jewish in character, more in continuity with the "conservative" Jewish Christianity of Jerusalem than it was even with the Pauline mission. For example, the church father Ambrosiaster, writing about 350 C.E., noted that Roman Christianity was established with a Jewish bent.[31] In fact, the book of Romans itself probably indicates that the relationship between Jew and Gentile was a relevant, although perhaps not divisive, issue for the Roman church of the late 50s.

It is interesting that while *1 Clement* shows strong awareness of Hebrews, Clement does not seem to have agreed with all of Hebrews's admonitions. For example, using language that strongly echoes Heb. 12:17, Clement argues that God consistently gives a "place of repentance" to those who turn to him, thus seeming to contradict Hebrews. Even more significant, Clement refers to Jewish priests and Levites as if they legitimately serve the altar *currently*, giving no indication that their service has stopped or is now inappropriate (*1 Clem.* 32.2). He uses the hierarchy and functioning of the Jerusalem temple as a model for church structure without arguing against it in any way (40.5; 41.2).

First Peter utilizes a great deal of cultic imagery in its argument and was most likely written from Rome. Although written to Gentile believers (1 Pet. 2:10), it refers to them as a "royal priesthood" (2:5, 9) that offers spiritual sacrifices to God (cf. Heb. 13:15). More than many other writings of the New Testament, sacrificial imagery plays a prominent role in 1 Peter (e.g., 1:2, 19; 2:5, 24). The Shepherd of Hermas also at many points seems more Jewish than Christian. Many even believe it to have incorporated originally Jewish material. In short, it is plausible to see Roman Christianity in slightly greater continuity with mainstream Judaism than some of Paul's heirs were.

We can imagine that many Christians at one time saw no tension between relying on both Levitical sacrifices *and* Christ's death as a sacrifice. Indeed, the book of Acts implies that many Jewish Christians did not think Christ's death nullified the sacrificial system in any way.[32] We can imagine that many believed that the Levitical system not only provided legitimate means of atonement *in addition to that provided by Christ* but perhaps even that it was essential for complete and continuous atonement (cf. Acts 13:38; Gal. 2:16). It is reasonable to assume that those Gentiles who converted under the influence of such Christians similarly saw no contradiction between the validity of the Levitical cultus and trusting in Christ.

One reason the predominantly Gentile Christianity at Rome may have retained a strongly Jewish character is the fact that many Gentiles in Rome found Judaism itself attractive. Although the term "God-fearer" in Acts may very well be a phrase coined by its author, surely it was not uncommon for Gentiles to associate themselves with Jewish synagogues here and there. Indeed, Gentiles who were connected with Jewish synagogues before they became Christians might no doubt easily find their way back under pressure or if they lost confidence in the message of Christianity.

All in all, the evidence is fairly good to show that many Romans of the first century found Judaism attractive. We alluded above to the fact that the consul Flavius Clemens was put to death ostensibly for wandering into "Jewish ways."[33] He seems to be just one example of a number of upper-class Romans, particularly women, who found Judaism attractive. The satirist Seneca, writing during the life of Paul, noted that "The custom of this most wicked race [i.e. the Jews] grew so strong that it has now been received through all lands. The conquered gave their laws to the victors."[34] The Roman historian Tacitus, writing in the early second century, speaks with scorn of those who convert to Judaism, making it clear that such conversions were a known element of his world (*Histories* 5.5).

> Those who have been converted to their [Jewish] custom take over the same practice [i.e., circumcising to distinguish themselves from everyone else], and the first thing they are taught is to despise the gods, to disown their homeland, and to consider their parents, children, and brothers as unimportant.
> —Tacitus, *Histories* 5.5

He abhors those who have abandoned the Roman religion and contributed their resources to such an extent that the wealth of Jews has become great around the world.

The satirist Juvenal, writing at the same time, has scathing remarks of a similar nature for the Roman father that leads his son so far in the direction of Judaism that the son decides to go one step further and be circumcised (*Satires* 14.96–106). These scattered comments throughout Roman literature indicate that many Romans were attracted to Judaism in a significant way. It is probably from this "pool" that most of the Gentile converts to Christianity were at least initially drawn.

Therefore, it is not unreasonable to suggest that if the confidence of many Gentile Christians were to waver, a turn or return to the synagogue could be as reasonable an alternative as it would have been for a Jewish Christian—especially if Christianity in Rome had a more conservative Jewish flavor anyway. After all, the Jewish community in Rome had not suffered during the persecution under Nero, only the Christian community had. In addition, since Clement mentions jealousy as the reason for Peter and Paul's deaths at that time, mainstream Jews may have participated in turning Jewish Christians over to the authorities at that time (*1 Clem.* 5). Controversy between the synagogues of Rome over Christianity probably dates back at least to the year 49 C.E., when Claudius expelled the Jews from Rome. It is not unreasonable to suggest that under the threat of persecution in general some Jewish synagogues might begin to exert pressure on Christians in Rome. In short, any number of factors could have facilitated a turn toward mainstream Judaism in a context in which one feared that persecution was just on the horizon—not only for Jewish Christians but Gentile Christians as well.

In the end we simply do not know the details of the audience's situation. We can only make educated guesses about the main elements in the equation. Their main problem was waning confidence in the Christian message. A number of factors probably played into this wavering: the delay of Christ's return, the pull of mainstream Judaism, and especially the anticipation of persecution. The author saw the Levitical cultus in particular as holding a competing claim for their allegiance. Yet he never ended his expositions with a command not to rely on the Old Testament sacrificial system. Rather, he focused on the confidence the audience could have in Christ's atonement and on the boldness with which they might approach God's heavenly presence (especially Heb. 4:14–16; 10:18–23).

CONCLUSION

Whatever specific details we give to the situation behind Hebrews, it seems fairly certain that two principal elements stand behind its composition. The most immediate problem is their waning confidence in the certainty of the salvation provided by Christ. While the delay of Christ's return might very well have been part of the problem, the primary factor seems to have been impending hardship and persecution. Such hardship could range from alienation and disgrace to the seizure of property, exile, and perhaps even potential martyrdom.

Christians were liable to prosecution by Roman law on several different charges. They could be accused of unlawful assembly or, during the reign of Domitian, be charged with failure to pay the Jewish tax—even if they were not Jewish. They could be charged with atheism for failure to participate in the state religion. Various aspects of Hebrews's exhortations could be taken as allusions to any one of these consequences.

On the other hand, the Levitical sacrificial system seems in some way to provide a live alternative to the community's faith in Christ. While reliance on Levitical means of atonement is not the focus of the epistle's exhortations, it nonetheless is what the author argues against to bolster their confidence in the effectiveness of Christ's sacrificial death. This fact implies that while their confidence in Christ is waning, they remain confident in the Old Testament and its sacrificial system. Some are even drawn by "strange teaching" involving Levitical meals thought to have atoning value.

Several contexts could account for these factors. William Lane has suggested that Hebrews was written to Jewish Christians at Rome near the beginning of Nero's persecution (i.e., before 64 C.E.). Such a hypothesis accounts for overtones of hardship and dates the epistle before any Christians at Rome had been put to death (Heb. 12:4). It takes a number of comments in what seems to be their most straightforward sense, such as statements in the present tense about the offering of Levitical sacrifices. The suggestion of a Jewish Christian audience is also a natural explanation for arguments against the Levitical cultus, since a Jewish Christian might very well struggle with reliance on the Levitical system.

On the other hand, while this hypothesis is cogent and has many strong points it may not do justice to the subtlety of Hebrews. For example, the author never mentions the Jerusalem temple, an odd fact if it is in view. His language of the wilderness tabernacle and of obscure "foods" do not likely relate to any literal operation in the Jerusalem temple. And this hypothesis does not take seriously enough the likelihood that the church at Rome was predominantly Gentile in composition. Further, the theology of Hebrews arguably fits better in the period when John and other post–70 C.E. documents were being written than it does with the writings of the early 60s. The way in which Clement refers to Hebrews fits better with a sermon sent within the last ten years than one sent forty years previously.

For these reasons we have put forward the suggestion that Hebrews was written to a predominantly Gentile church in Rome during the earlier part of Domitian's reign (81–96 C.E.). While a persecution of Christians under Domitian is not as well documented as one under Nero, we have good reason to believe Christians experienced some hardship and persecution in the general way that Hebrews seems to propose. We have tried to show that the rhetoric of Hebrews would have made sense given the character of Gentile Christianity in Rome in the late first century. In the context of an emperor who styled himself as "Lord and God," Hebrews rhetoric regarding Christ as Son of God and high priest, not to mention the maintenance of our Christian *confession*, would have been a not-so-subtle reminder of the audience's proper loyalties.

We could mention any number of other suggestions that various scholars have made over the years. Most combine one or more of the elements we have already mentioned. Most follow Lane in picturing a Jewish audience. Some emphasize external persecution while others focus on a return to mainstream Judaism. Most see a waning confidence in the Christian message as a main factor.

Almost any conceivable destination has been suggested at some time or another. In general, destinations other than Rome lack the kind of evidence one would need in order to make a compelling case. Jerusalem, though unlikely for many reasons, was the main contender throughout most of church history because of Hebrews's arguments against reliance on the Levitical cultus. Perhaps the best suggestion outside of Rome is that it was written to somewhere in Asia Minor, such as the Lycus Valley. From Colossians and the letters of Ignatius we know that some Gentiles in these areas kept the Jewish law to a surprising degree.

In the end, the situation behind Hebrews, as the name of its author, was well known to its audience—so well known, in fact, that the author omitted the kinds of details that might really fine-tune our understanding of its argument and rhetoric. We have tried our best to suggest some plausible alternatives, and we have had more evidence to go on than we would in tackling an issue like the authorship of the letter/sermon. Ultimately, however, we must say to some degree what the church father Origen said about its author: "the truth is, God knows."[35]

Conclusion

We set out to capture the thought and rhetoric of Hebrews by looking at the story world behind it and the way it argues from that story—what I like to call the "rhetorical world" of Hebrews. Using the categories of event, character, and setting, we explored the way Hebrews assigns rhetorical significance to each in order to move its audience to a certain course of action, namely, continued faithfulness to the Christian confession. We also conducted this exploration with a view to the way the author has arranged the "surface" of his argument in the text, such as the way he begins in Heb. 1 with a hymnic celebration of the now enthroned Son of God. This method allowed us to address questions of background from a balanced perspective.

The key *event* with which Hebrews is concerned is the sacrifice/high priestly offering of Christ, an event that Hebrews overlays with metaphor after metaphor. The author transformed Christ's crucifixion and his entrance into heaven (which the author probably conceived literally) into an atoning sacrifice taken into the true, heavenly sanctuary by Christ, a priest after the order of Melchizedek. The author assigns ultimate rhetorical significance to this event. It becomes the sacrifice to end all sacrifices, a covenant-making act that ends the "old" covenant mediated to Israel through angels and Moses.

The author argues that it is a different kind of sacrifice from the endlessly offered sacrifices of the old covenant. Here the *setting* of the sacrifice comes into play. The sacrifices of the old covenant were offered in an earthly sanctuary that at best could only cleanse physical flesh. In contrast, Christ offers his sacrifice in heaven in the true sanctuary, a place made up of a different kind of "stuff" than earth and the creation. This setting of the sacrifice makes it effectual for the cleansing of spirit and the removal of a consciousness of sin. The many and various sacrifices of the old covenant were only shadowy illustrations of this one truly effective sacrifice offered by Christ.

The author makes this complex argument because the Levitical system in some way stands as the audience's main alternative to Christ. The focal problem Hebrews addresses is a waning confidence in the Christian confession. At the end of each of his expositions, he draws one of two basic conclusions. One is the certainty and definiteness of Christ's atonement. Both before and after the central teaching section of the epistle (Heb. 5:1–10:18) he encourages his audience to approach God boldly for grace to help in time of need. When he takes this tact, he affirms strongly that the audience has access through Christ to sacred space and true atonement.

In several other places, the author concludes his teaching with a different tactic. He issues a stern warning to anyone who would neglect the salvation provided by Christ. If God punished those who broke the law of Moses, those who break the "law" of Christ are in serious trouble. In both these ways, the author strongly encourages the audience to remain true to their Christian confession.

The audience has not accidentally or casually drifted away from their confidence. They have not just slowly lost hope because of the delay in Christ's return or a long-term loss of honor. These things may be factors in the equation, but they are not the central factors. In the examples the author gives from some of the *characters* in the plot of salvation history, we see that a real situation involving external pressure is the catalyst for the audience's crisis of faithfulness. On the one hand, some of the examples do simply reinforce a general need for faithfulness. The wilderness generation serves as a shameful example of the type of person who does not persist in faithfulness to God's word. Their corpses fell in the desert. Yet in many other cases, consistent themes emerge in the way the author presents the characters of the plot as examples.

For example, Esau sold his birthright *for food* (Heb. 12:16). In the same way, Heb. 13:9 indicates that some in the community are tempted to rely on Levitical *foods* of some sort for confident atonement. Examples of faithfulness from Abel to Christ evoke images of martyrdom, although the audience has not yet faced death in their current crisis (12:4). Other examples have connotations of persecution from pagan authorities, such as the "edict of the king" scorned by Moses' parents (11:23). Jesus himself is the ultimate example of a son who "learned obedience through the things he suffered" (5:8). This often vague rhetoric implies a situation in which the audience fears a persecution looming on the horizon, perhaps one that has already begun. On the whole, we suggested that the earlier part of Domitian's reign in Rome is a good candidate for this ambiance.

Therefore, with the intent of inspiring his audience to endurance, the author crafted the text of Hebrews to move them to reaffirm values they once held and to be firm in the continuance of their faith. He wants them to maintain their public confession of Christ and hope in him. He intertwines his exposition of the story with pointed exhortations to his audience, holding their attention while constantly leading them back to the point at hand.

After a brief introduction that encapsulates the main themes of the sermon (1:1–4), he begins with a hymnic celebration of Christ's exaltation to God's right hand as cosmic Son of God. Given the association the author makes between angels and the old covenant, this celebration implies the accomplishment of salvation and the definitive greatness of Christ. The angels were the overarching mediators between God and the earth during the old covenant. This role is coming to an end as Christ becomes God's definitive mediator to his true people.

In Heb. 2 the author recounts the significance of Christ's exaltation above the angels. He rehearses the place God intended humanity to have in the creation and shows how God used Christ to free us from enslavement to death and the devil in the created realm. In Christ we also have hope to attain a glory above the angels. The chapter ends with what are arguably the key verses of Hebrews: 2:17–18. God made Christ like humanity so that he might be a faithful and merciful high priest who atones for the sins of the people.

With the thread of the high priestly argument begun, the author turns to Moses, the one to whom the angels delivered the law on earth. While Moses was a servant among God's people, Christ was a son in God's household. The author uses the shameful disbelief of the wilderness generation under Moses to warn the audience of what will happen if they disbelieve under Christ's charge. He ends the discussion with a pointed message about the discerning judgment of God's word (4:12–13).

If the angels were God's overall mediators to the created realm and Moses was the one to whom the law in general was delivered, Heb. 5 turns specifically to the priestly functions of the law. If Christ will replace the Levitical sacrificial system, he must be a priest that replaces the Levitical priests. Hebrews 5 and 7 argue that he is such a superior priest, a priest after the order of Melchizedek. This priestly order, defined by its indestructible life, is far superior to the Levitical order. The arrival of such a priest entails the end of the Levitical system and the law of which it was the foundation.

It is in the middle of this argument that the author pauses to give his strongest and most pointed warning to the audience. They are in danger of permanently missing out on the salvation Christ has provided. They have received the constant rain of God's grace, yet if they bear thorns and thistles they will be cast into the fire. The author is confident they will renew their commitment to Christ, using the example of Abraham to underline *God's* faithfulness to his promises.

Hebrews 8–10 form the heart of the argument. In these chapters the author contrasts the sacrifice and heavenly sanctuary of Christ with the sacrifices and earthly tent of the Levitical system. He argues that the new covenant mediated through Christ is effective and final where the old covenant was ineffective and endless. "With one offering," he says, Christ "has perfected forever those who are being made holy" (10:14). The sacrifices of the old covenant are thus no longer needed (cf. v. 18).

With this main point made, the remaining chapters of Hebrews encourage the audience to follow through in their faithfulness to Christ. The remainder of

Heb. 10 encourages them to remember their past faithfulness and reiterates the frightening prospect of destruction for those who shrink back (10:39). Hebrews 11 bombards the audience with pertinent examples of faithfulness, a "cloud of witnesses" that remained faithful and despised the shame of their persecutors (12:1–2). Hebrews 12 uses the metaphor of sonship to urge the audience to submit to God's discipline and training. This chapter ends with some of the most powerful and apocalyptic images of judgment in the sermon. Hebrews 13 then ends the book with a letter's conclusion, reiterating in its own way many of the themes found in the preceding chapters.

Even at the end of our study we lack definite answers to most of the epistle's great unknowns. We suspect that the author was a Greek speaker, probably a Jew, who had enjoyed the education afforded to only a few. We do not know his name. Rome is a good guess for the destination, and we argued for a predominantly Gentile audience during the early reign of Domitian—but these are educated guesses rather than certainties.

We have almost no sense of its point of origin, although the name of Timothy could suggest Asia Minor (13:23). Its background of thought has hints of Middle Platonism and a touch of apocalyptic, but more than anything our author is a Christian. He shows greater affinities to Paul than he does to any non-Christian author of any sort. All in all, the most interesting thing about our answers to these questions is the fact that we were able to interpret Hebrews to a great degree without knowing them.

It would be nice to know the effect this ancient sermon had on its first audience. We would like to know if they renewed their commitment to Christ and if they relinquished their attraction to the Levitical system. We would like to know if any did eventually resist sin to the point of blood. If Hebrews was written at the time and place we have suggested, its imagery did reverberate in the mind of Clement of Rome, even if he did not entirely agree with its teaching. One wonders if it influenced the way he thought about the altar from which we as Christians have authority to eat (Heb. 13:10). It is fascinating to wonder if Hebrews ironically inspired his notion that the celebration of the Eucharist by the bishop was the offering of a sacrifice (1 Clem. 4:4). While we will never know the specific repercussions this astounding sermon had at that time, its message of true cleansing and of unhindered access to God remain strong encouragements for Christians today.

Notes

Introduction

1. Hebrews is more a *sermon* than an "epistle," and its audience was not likely made up of Aramaic-speaking Jews. Indeed, it is quite possible that the audience was predominantly Gentile.
2. Greek participles and nouns have a masculine, feminine, or neuter gender to them. In Heb. 11:32, the author uses a masculine singular participle in reference to himself.
3. The author quotes the Jewish Scriptures from their Greek translation, the Septuagint. At more than one point, he argues from some aspect of the *Greek* text where the Hebrew is worded differently (e.g., Heb. 1:6; 10:5). Hebrews 9:16-17 also makes a point the author could not have made in Hebrew—only in Greek does the word *covenant* also mean a "will." In short, Hebrews gives us no indication that its author even knew Hebrew or Aramaic.
4. The same phrase appears in Acts 13:15 for a short sermon Paul gives in a synagogue. If Hebrews were a straightforward letter, it surely would have begun with an identification of the author and audience in keeping with ancient letter style.
5. In fact, not all commentators on Hebrews even agree on some of the "basics" just mentioned.
6. For an excellent introduction to narrative criticism, see Mark A. Powell's *What Is Narrative Criticism?* (Minneapolis: Fortress, 1990).
7. For this reason the ultimate goals of narrative criticism are somewhat ambiguous. The fundamental orientation of most who practice its method is a-historical, since they claim largely to "bracket" historical factors in interpretation. Yet there is no such thing as a-historical interpretation. All words receive their meaning from a context, particularly the context of the reader. Therefore, those narrative critics who cut themselves loose from the original historical context are actually practicing a variety of reader-response criticism (cf. Stephen Moore, *Literary Criticism and the Gospels: The Theoretical Challenge* [New Haven, Conn.: Yale University Press, 1989], 73). Reader-response criticism is an approach to interpretation that looks to the readers of a text for its meaning rather than to its author or historical context. Because the "responses" of each reader will differ

from one another, a text comes to have as many meanings as there are readers. Historical-critical interpretation is not immune from this dynamic, although I would argue that the goal is intact enough for it to be a legitimate enterprise.

8. A number of recent studies have applied this basic realization in one way or another to Paul's letters. Richard B. Hays, whose work was groundbreaking in this respect, analyzed the argument in Galatians from this standpoint (*The Faith of Jesus Christ* [Chico, Calif.: Scholars Press, 1983]). Norman R. Petersen took a slightly different narrative approach in his exploration of Philemon, focusing on the immediate historical situation behind its writing rather than the plot of salvation history in general (*Rediscovering Paul: Philemon and the Sociology of Paul's Narrative World* [Philadelphia: Fortress, 1985]). Ben Witherington III attempted to capture Paul's thought world from this standpoint in *Paul's Narrative Thought World: The Tapestry of Tragedy and Triumph* (Louisville, Ky.: Westminster John Knox, 1994). And N. T. Wright has advocated this approach to early Christian thought in general (e.g., *The New Testament and the People of God* [Minneapolis: Fortress, 1992])

9. In reality I prefer the phrase "rhetorical world" to "thought world." By rhetorical world I refer to the story world of Hebrews in combination with the rhetoric that proceeds from it. Thus while a Gospel is a "story-as-discoursed" in a narrative, Paul's letters and Hebrews are "stories-as-discoursed" in rhetoric.

Chapter 1: The Story World of Hebrews

1. As the introduction notes, the original Greek text of Heb. 11:32 strongly implies that the author of Hebrews was male, although this aspect of the text does not show up in an English translation.

2. The Greek word *ouranos* translates as both "heaven" and "sky"—a distinction that has more to do with our current worldview than with that of the biblical texts. The author of Hebrews probably pictured a universe in which one passed upward through multiple layers of heaven, including what we call the sky, until one finally arrived at the highest heaven, where God's throne was located (cf. Heb. 4:14; 7:26).

3. The nature of the heavenly tabernacle in Hebrews is a matter of significant debate. See chapter 5 for a discussion of the possibilities.

4. For many years scholars assumed this contrast was Platonic and that the author of Hebrews was heavily dependent on traditions like those found in the Jewish philosopher Philo. We are now much more cautious about making such connections, since apocalyptic literature often has similar contrasts. For a scholarly treatment of the topic, see Lincoln Hurst's *The Epistle to the Hebrews: Its Background of Thought* (SNTSMS 65; Cambridge: Cambridge University Press, 1990), 7–42.

5. The author is citing Ps. 102:26. All translations are mine unless otherwise noted.

6. I take this statement to be a somewhat poetic exaggeration.

7. One should be careful not to assume that Hebrews uses these terms in the same way Paul does.

8. Hebrews 9:14 is interesting in its contrast between the cleansing of the flesh by the blood of goats and bulls and the blood of Christ offered "through an eternal spirit." Many commentators understand this phrase in terms of the Holy Spirit, a conclusion with which I do not completely disagree. The focus of the contrast, however, is between the two different media—the one physical and the other spiritual.

9. Someone might notice that the heavenly tabernacle appears to need cleansing as well in 9:23, but we should not take the heavenly consecration here too literally.

The author is really speaking metaphorically of the need for human sin to be cleansed. His highly metaphorical argument requires him to place this purification in the heavenly realm.

10. Many commentators and translations of Heb. 8:5 translate the word *upodeigma* as "copy," giving a distinctively Platonic feel to the verse. However, Lincoln Hurst has argued convincingly that the word does not generally have this meaning in the corpus of ancient Greek literature ("How 'Platonic' Are Heb. viii.5 and ix.23f?," *JTS* 34 [1983]: 156–68). The New Revised Standard Version has followed his lead by translating the word as "a sketch." The same word is translated "example" in 4:11.

11. It is appropriate to speak of Hebrews's recipients as an "audience" for at least two reasons. On the one hand, most ancient persons were illiterate. Accordingly, we should picture someone reading Hebrews aloud to a Christian gathering. We should not think of individuals reading it as we do, each with his or her own copy in hand. Second, a good number of scholars believe Hebrews was a homily or short sermon. The author calls it a "word of exhortation" in 13:22, a phrase Acts 13:15 uses in reference to a synagogue homily.

12. For example, 2:1; 3:12–14; 4:1, 11, 14–16; 6:4–6, 11; 10:19–22, 32–39; 12:1–2, 12–13, 15, 25. George H. Guthrie has explored the alternation between exhortation and exposition in Hebrews in significant detail. See *The Structure of Hebrews: A Text–Linguistic Analysis* (SNT 73; Leiden: E. J. Brill, 1994), 9–10, 112–47.

13. Both "removal" and "transformation" are possible translations of the Greek word *metathesis*, which occurs in 12:27. We will "fall off the log" on the side of removal in chapter 2.

14. Hebrews 1:3 bears a strong resemblance to Wis. 7:26.

15. So also Mary R. D'Angelo, *Moses in the Letter to the Hebrews* (SBLDS 42; Missoula, Mont.: Scholars Press, 1979), 243–46.

16. The same word and form is used in 8:6 and 7:11: *nenomothetetai*—"it has been instituted by law."

17. It is often difficult for Christians to conceive of Christ's Sonship in terms of an office or an appointment. It is much easier to think of the phrase "Son of God" in terms of Christ's divinity as the second person of the Trinity. Indeed, this is how the phrase comes to be used in the church. Yet the early Christians understood it more in terms of its use in the Jewish Scriptures (i.e., the Christian Old Testament). In this context, "Son of God" can be a title referring to God's anointed king. When God bestows the name "Son" on Christ in Heb. 1:5, he is enthroning him as king.

18. To call Christ's death a sacrifice is a metaphor in and of itself. The capital punishment of a human on a cross is compared to the slaughter of an animal on an altar.

19. See chapter 5 for a further discussion of Christ's high priesthood.

20. Not all agree with this interpretation. See my article, "The Celebration of the Enthroned Son: The Catena of Hebrews 1:5–14," *JBL* 120 (2001): 469–85.

21. "The Exegetical Method of the Epistle to the Hebrews," *CJT* 5 (1959): 47.

22. The phrase *brachi ti* could be taken either spatially—"a little lower"—or temporally—"for a little while." The context indicates that the latter is more appropriate.

23. Of course, humans play key roles in the numerous "subplots" of the story. For example, we could easily describe the situation of the community to which Hebrews is addressed as a self-contained story, much as Norman R. Petersen has done with Paul's letter to Philemon in *Rediscovering Paul: Philemon and the Sociology of Paul's Narrative World* (Philadelphia: Fortress, 1985).

24. To say that Christ was the one "through whom" God made the worlds sounds conspicuously like language used of God's wisdom and his word in the Jewish literature of the time (e.g., Wis. 9:1–2).

25. See chapter 3 for further discussion.

26. For example, 1:1–2, 5–8; 2:2–3, 6, 12–13; 3:7; 4:2–4, 7, 12–13; 5:5–6, 11; 6:1; 10:5, 15; 13:7.

27. In this time period, Jewish thinkers like Philo of Alexandria had synthesized this imagery in the Jewish Scriptures with Stoic thinking about the *logos* ("word") and a bit of Plato thrown in to boot. The Stoics saw the *logos* as the ordering principle of the universe, similar to the concept of Fate. It was pointless to fight against the inevitable, so one should be content with whatever lot divine reason had in store for you. Certain segments of early Christianity, including Hebrews, drew on these rich traditions as they attempted to describe the significance of Christ for God's creation.

28. An interestingly similar sentiment is found in Wis. 18:15–16 with regard to the angel of death in the story of the exodus: "your all powerful word wandered from heaven, . . . a stern warrior carrying a sharp sword—your genuine command."

29. This statement is probably an allusion to the seven brothers of 2 Macc. 7. For a full study of Heb. 11 as an "example list," see Michael R. Cosby, *The Rhetorical Composition and Function of Hebrews 11: In Light of Example Lists of Antiquity* (Macon, Ga.: Mercer University Press, 1988). See also Pamela M. Eisenbaum, *The Jewish Heroes of Christian History: Hebrews 11 in Literary Context* (SBLDS 156; Atlanta: Scholars Press, 1997).

30. There has been some debate over the exact nuance of the phrase "out of death" in 5:7. I agree with Harold W. Attridge that this verse is referring to Jesus' faith that God could raise him from the dead. See "'Heard Because of His Reverence' (Heb 5:7)," *JBL* 98 (1979): 90–93.

31. See n. 17. Hebrews is the only New Testament writing that places Christ's enthronement at the time of his session to God's right hand. Acts 13:33 and Rom. 1:4 roughly indicate the same timing, and the use of the title "Lord" seems to follow the same basic pattern (see Acts 2:36; Rom. 10:9; Phil. 2:9–11). As Attridge has pointed out, Hebrews also has imagery implying that Christ was son (5:8) and high priest (v. 7) before his death (*The Epistle to the Hebrews: A Commentary on the Epistle to the Hebrews* [Philadelphia: Fortress, 1989], 146–47). These minor tensions are due to the heavily metaphorical nature of the author's argument and do not nullify that the focus of these titles is Christ in his exaltation.

32. Hebrews's designation of Christ as a priest after the order of Melchizedek is yet another issue about which scholars have debated extensively. Whom does the author understand Melchizedek to be? We can clarify the issue significantly if we realize that the author is not asking who Melchizedek was but what a priest *after the order of Melchizedek* might be. He is not primarily interpreting the text of Gen. 14 but Ps. 110:4, where he believes the Messiah is designated as a priest after the order of Melchizedek. The author only turns to the Genesis text to define what a priest after the order of Melchizedek is, namely, a king-priest who does not come from a Levitical genealogy and whose office as priest does not end. Christ and only Christ has ever been qualified for such an office. See chapter 5 for further discussion.

Chapter 2: Humanity's Problem and Christ's Solution

1. The light Paul's thinking sheds on Hebrews's argument coupled with the fact that a "Timothy" is somehow associated with its author (Heb. 13:23) makes it very likely, in our opinion, that the author was associated with the Pauline circle and

perhaps that the audience was one of the many communities that came under Paul's influence during the course of his ministry.

2. For a basic overview of structuralism, see Daniel Patte, *What Is Structural Exegesis?* (Philadelphia: Fortress, 1976). Even more helpful is N. T. Wright's overview in *The New Testament and the People of God* (Minneapolis: Fortress, 1992), 69–73.

3. In the technical lingo of structuralism, God is the *sender* and humanity the *receiver*. The *object* being sent is glory and honor. The created order is the *agent* by way of which God is sending glory and honor. The human spirit with its capacity for immortality should have contributed to humanity's honor, not to mention the creatures humanity was to rule. These were potential *helpers* in this "initial sequence" of the plot. Unfortunately, the devil as the *opponent* overcame the helpers and prevented the agent from conveying the object to the receiver. That is, humans did not receive glory and honor in the created realm.

4. In keeping with the fact that Hebrews does not fully tell the beginnings of the plot, it is difficult to know for certain that humanity's glory could ever have occurred in the earthly realm. The fact that Ps. 8 takes Gen. 1 somewhat literally does not mean that the author of Hebrews understood it that way. In other words, Hebrews may not have equated the glory and honor God meant for humanity with the glory and honor of the creation story.

5. Some of those who deny that Ps. 8 in Heb. 2:6–8 relates to humans as well as to Christ include Ernst Käsemann, *The Wandering People of God: An Investigation of the Letter to the Hebrews* (Minneapolis: Augsburg, 1984 [1957]), 122–26; Harold W. Attridge, *The Epistle to the Hebrews* (Philadelphia: Fortress, 1989), 70–75; Donald A. Hagner, *Hebrews* (Peabody, Mass.: Hendrickson, 1990), 44–47; and George H. Guthrie, *Hebrews* (Grand Rapids: Zondervan, 1998), 96.

6. Although the Greek behind the Gospel's use of this phrase is consistently "the son of *the* man," whereas here it is merely "the son of man." Cf. William L. Lane, *Hebrews 1–8* (Dallas: Word, 1991), 47.

7. Probably understood in reference to all who partake of Christ whether Jew or Gentile (3:14).

8. Most commentators see in this verse a reference to the *Holy* Spirit rather than Christ's spirit. The two options probably do not completely exclude each other, however.

9. Philo, like almost everyone in his day, probably did not believe that God had created the world out of nothing.

10. It is difficult to be certain because the author's later allusion to Adam does not make any mention of the devil (Wis. 10:1–2).

11. The Wisdom of Solomon is perhaps the earliest example in Jewish literature where this serpent is equated with the devil. The Genesis story itself does not make such an equation. In fact, it is highly unlikely that Israelite religion had any concept of any "Satan" at the time when the Adam and Eve story was first given written form (e.g., compare 2 Sam. 24:1 with the later 1 Chr. 21:1).

12. *Life* 12–17.

13. Many scholars have missed the import of Heb. 5:7 because they equate it with Jesus' prayer to avoid death in the Garden of Gethsemane. Jesus' prayer, however, makes no sense as a prayer to avoid death, since God did not "hear" that request. His prayer is rather to be raised from the dead, to be saved "out of" death. Cf. Harold W. Attridge, "'Heard Because of His Reverence' (Heb 5:7)," *JBL* 98 (1979): 90–93.

14. See, for example, J. Christiaan Beker, *Paul the Apostle: The Triumph of God in Life*

and Thought (Edinburgh: T & T Clark, 1980), 189–92; 213–34. Hints that such powers stand behind the power of sin and death in Paul's thought can be found in such places as Rom. 8:38–39; 1 Cor. 2:8; 15:24–26 (cf. Eph. 1:21; 6:12; Col. 1:16).

15. Paul's end to the story actually seems very similar to this proposal. On the other hand, Hebrews seems to take a somewhat different tact.

16. While all humanity was initially meant to experience glory and honor, Christ leads "sons" to glory only in the end.

17. Enoch is a possible exception (cf. Heb. 11:5).

18. Hebrews 5:7 seems to point to the latter.

19. See chapter 5 for a defense of this position.

20. Hebrews's understanding of the conscience is quite different from ours. On the one hand, it has a rational overtone, as in our word *consciousness*. Hebrews 10:2–3 indicate that the word is roughly synonymous to the word *remembrance*. To "cleanse the conscience" could thus be shorthand for "to cleanse your sins so that you have no sin of which you are conscious." On the other hand, it is also possible that the author views the conscience as the part of one's spirit that becomes contaminated by sin, just as the flesh is that which is defiled physically.

21. Wilfrid Stott is an example of the first position: "The Conception of 'Offering' in the Epistle to the Hebrews," *NTS* 9 (1962–63): 62–67. Walter E. Brooks illustrates the latter: "The Perpetuity of Christ's Sacrifice in the Epistle to the Hebrews," *JBL* 89 (1970): 205–14.

22. So also David A. deSilva, *Perseverance in Gratitude: A Socio-Rhetorical Commentary on the Epistle "to the Hebrews"* (Grand Rapids: Eerdmans, 2000), 218.

23. The parallelism between cleansing and perfection in Heb. 10:1–2 highlights the centrality of cleansing in the "completion" or "perfection" of our humanness. For a full-scale treatment of perfection language in Hebrews, see David G. Peterson, *Hebrews and Perfection: An Examination of the Concept of Perfection in the "Epistle to the Hebrews"* (Cambridge: Cambridge University Press, 1982).

24. While to say we have arrived to the place of "spirits of the righteous that have been perfected" could be a statement of expectation—about something that is so certain that we can already say we have arrived in heaven even though our entrance is really still to come—we take it also to mean that our spirits already enjoy participation in the heavenly realm while we are still on earth.

25. The Old Testament conception of soul relates to the entirety of a person as a living being. In Gen. 2, God takes dust (=earth), breathes into it (=spirit), and Adam becomes a living *soul* (Gen. 2:7).

26. *Anago* rather than *anistemi*.

27. Hebrews gives at least one other hint that our spirits attain to heaven even while we are still in our bodies. Our spirits are presumably part of what God will shake when he judges the created realm. The imagery of 12:18–29 entails a *present* warning to those in the audience that their spirits are still liable to God's judgment even though they have already arrived at the heavenly Jerusalem. So Lane, *Hebrews 1–8*, 482–83.

28. The ability of the author of Hebrews to mix such stereotypically "apocalyptic" features with other stereotypically "philosophical" ones demonstrates powerfully that these categories are not mutually exclusive. The stereotypes by which a previous generation used to pigeonhole Hebrews's thought often had more to do with modern presuppositions than with ancient categories of thought.

Chapter 3: The Celebration of the Enthroned Son

1. A more in-depth treatment of this topic appeared in *JBL* 120 (2001): 469–85 under the same title as this chapter.

2. For example, Philip E. Hughes's commentary, *A Commentary on the Epistle to the Hebrews* (Grand Rapids: Eerdmans, 1977).

3. For example, Ernst Käsemann, *The Wandering People of God* (Minneapolis: Augsburg, 1984 [1961]), 169–70.

4. *The Epistle to the Hebrews*, Hermeneia (Philadelphia: Fortress, 1989), 54–55.

5. Documents found at Qumran, 4QTestim and 4QFlor, are largely collections of quotations from the Old Testament.

6. *CJT* 5 (1959): 47.

7. For further explanation of this paragraph, see chapter 1.

8. Lincoln Hurst has attempted to work out the specific details of Caird's suggestion in an article in Caird's honor: "The Christology of Heb 1 and 2," in *The Glory of Christ in the New Testament: Studies in Christology in Memory of George Bradford Caird*, L. D. Hurst and N. T. Wright, eds. (Oxford: Clarendon, 1987), 151–64. His article does not seem to have had much impact on the discussion, perhaps because he focuses too much on the individual citations themselves rather than on the way the catena fits in with the broader scheme of Hebrews' rhetoric.

9. See chapter 1 for a basic presentation of this position and chapter 5 for a more detailed argument.

10. For example, Phil. 2:6–11; Col. 1:15–20.

11. Ancient rhetoric attempted to persuade on three levels: (1) the "logical" (*logos*), which appealed to the audience's reason; (2) the "emotional" (*pathos*), which appealed to their emotions; and (3) the "personal" (*ethos*), which aimed at building trust between speaker and audience.

12. For example, Loren T. Stuckenbruck, *Angel Veneration and Christology: A Study in Early Judaism and in the Christology of the Apocalypse of John* (WUNT 70; Tübingen: Mohr [Siebeck], 1995), 128. So also Attridge, *Hebrews*, 50–51. We diminish the "logical distance" Stuckenbruck mentions if we bracket the exhortation of 2:1–4 and connect the train of thought from 1:14 to 2:5.

13. We should also keep in mind that the word *angel* did not always refer to a good being in first-century Judaism. Paul's writings quite commonly refer to evil angels (e.g., 1 Cor. 6:3; 2 Cor. 12:7), and he refers to the gods of the other nations as demons (1 Cor. 10:20). In contrast, Hebrews apparently refers only to good angels, those who were assigned to God's people.

14. This angel led Israel through the desert.

15. One of the greatest contributions of George H. Guthrie's work is to show that when the exhortations are removed from the exposition of Hebrews, a generally continuous argument can be seen (*The Structure of Hebrews: A Text-Linguistic Analysis* [Leiden: E. J. Brill, 1994], 112–26). Therefore, in one sense the thought of 2:5 continues on the heels of 1:14.

16. The following translation is taken from that of O. S. Wintermute in volume 2 of *The Old Testament Pseudepigrapha*, J. H. Charlesworth, ed. (New York: Doubleday, 1985), 35–142.

17. 1 QSa 2:8–9. In *The Dead Sea Scrolls Translated*, F. G. Martinez, trans. (Leiden: E. J. Brill, 1994).

18. An argument put forward by J. A. Fitzmyer in "A Feature of Qumran Angelology and the Angels of I Cor 11:10," *NTS* 4 (1957–58): 48–58. For a quite different argument, see Dale B. Martin, *The Corinthian Body* (New Haven, Conn.: Yale University Press, 1995), 229–49. Neither theory seems wholly satisfactory.

19. For an extensive bibliography on both of these positions, see Stuckenbruck, *Angel Veneration*, 124–25, n. 197–98. Some think Col. 2:18 refers to angel worship. The verse in Hebrews that comes closest to implying such a situation is Heb. 2:16.

20. So Attridge, *Hebrews*, 50; John P. Meier, "Structure and Theology in Heb 1,1–4," *Bib* 66 (1985): 168–89; and "Symmetry and Theology in Heb 1,5–14," *Bib* 66 (1985): 504–33.
21. The word *name* in Greek can refer to a role or office as well as to a proper name.
22. Jews in general did not use the terms "messiah" or "anointed one" in reference to God or a supernatural being who would come to earth as a human being. Rather, the term was used of a few, select roles or offices into which God placed special persons. Many Jews did expect that God would bring a political, royal messiah from the house of Judah to destroy Israel's foreign enemies and restore their political fortunes (e.g., *Pss. Sol.* 17). Other Jewish traditions also expected an anointed priest to come and restore appropriate temple worship (e.g., 1 QS 9:11).
23. For example, Sigmund Mowinckel, *The Psalms in Israel's Worship* (Oxford: Oxford University Press, 1962).
24. For a more detailed discussion, see my "Keeping His Appointment: Creation and Enthronement in the Epistle to the Hebrews," *JSNT* 66 (1996): 91–117.
25. 4QDeut. 32:43. See L. Hurst for discussion, "Christology," 158.
26. It is hard to capture the nuance of this verse in English because of distinctions we make that they did not. For example, the word *angelos* means both "messenger" and "angel" in Greek. Our language thus makes a clear distinction that was not so clear to them. We could say the same of the word *pneuma*, which meant both spirit and wind in Greek. While we would make a strong distinction between these two entities, they would not have.
27. There is some debate whether the psalmist understood the phrase to say "your throne is God" or "your throne, O God." Certainly the author of Hebrews understands it in the latter way.
28. We must always be careful when interpreting the meaning of a quotation from the Jewish Scriptures in the New Testament. New Testament authors were not at all limited to original meanings. In many cases the original meaning played almost no role in the use of Scripture. The most important question for New Testament interpretation is how a New Testament author reads a verse, not what it meant originally.
29. To see how one author connects this contrast to a Middle Platonic interpretation of Hebrews, see James W. Thompson, *The Beginnings of Christian Philosophy: The Epistle to the Hebrews* (CBQMS 13; Washington, D.C.: Catholic Biblical Association, 1982), 133.
30. See Hurst, "Christology," 160–62 for an attempt to explain them as verses the early church believed to be addressed to the Messiah.
31. The phrase "as a garment" has been added to the basic citation from the Jewish Scriptures. This addition serves to highlight the transitory nature of the earthly realm.
32. For an earlier treatment of this verse's importance in the New Testament, see David M. Hay, *Glory at the Right Hand: Ps 110:1 in Early Christianity* (SBLDS 18; Nashville: Abingdon, 1973).
33. The combination of the two in 1 Cor. 15:25 is subtle. While this verse refers to the exalted Christ as in Ps. 110:1, the statement that "all things are under his feet" comes from Ps. 8:6. It is also interesting that Eph. 1 connects Ps. 110:1 with Christ's rulership over angelic domains!

Chapter 4: Examples of Faith and Disbelief in the Old Covenant

1. For a treatment of the categories of honor and shame in Hebrews, see David A. deSilva, *Despising Shame: Honor Discourse and Community Maintenance in the Epistle to the Hebrews* (SBLDS 152; Atlanta: Scholars Press, 1995).

2. Technically, the term *Septuagint* refers only to the Greek translation of the first five books of the Hebrew Bible, the Pentateuch (see the *Letter of Aristeas*). However, for convenience and because of common practice I will refer to the entirety of the Greek Old Testament as the Septuagint.

3. For more on the way in which Hebrews interprets Old Testament Scriptures, see Simon J. Kistemaker, *The Psalm Citations in the Epistle to the Hebrews* (Amsterdam: Van Soest, 1961) and Richard N. Longenecker, *Biblical Exegesis in the Apostolic Period* (Grand Rapids: Eerdmans, 1975).

4. An interesting discussion of the way in which early Christians read the psalms as if Christ was speaking them can be found in Richard B. Hays's "Christ Prays the Psalms: Paul's Use of an Early Christian Exegetical Convention," in *The Future of Christology: Essays in Honor of Leander E. Keck* (Minneapolis: Fortress, 1993), 122–36.

5. See chapter 1.

6. Instead of the more usual term for creating, Hebrews uses a word in 11:3 that normally means to "mend." This fact may suggest that the author of Hebrews believed, like Philo, that God did not create the matter of the universe. Rather, creation was when he put chaotic, preexisting matter into order.

7. George H. Guthrie's text-linguistic analysis of Heb. 6 is very helpful for understanding the structure of Hebrews's argument at this point, *The Structure of Hebrews: A Text-Linguistic Analysis* (Leiden: E. J. Brill, 1994), 110–11.

8. Unlike the Sermon on the Mount (Matt. 5:33–37) or James (e.g., Jas. 5:12), Hebrews has no aversion to the idea of oath taking.

9. For a discussion of Hebrews's treatment of Moses and of his role in the Judaisms of the period in general, see Mary R. D'Angelo, *Moses in the Letter to the Hebrews* (SBLDS 42; Missoula, Mont: Scholars Press, 1979).

10. C. K. Barrett, "The Eschatology of the Epistle to the Hebrews," in *The Background of the New Testament and its Eschatology: Studies in Honour of C. H. Dodd* (Cambridge: Cambridge University Press, 1964), 372.

11. See chapter 6.

12. Although a different word for enemies is used in each case.

13. See chapter 6 for some suggestions.

14. Two important treatments of Heb. 11 are that of Michael R. Cosby, *The Rhetorical Composition and Function of Hebrews 11 in Light of Example Lists in Antiquity* (Macon, Ga.: Mercer University Press, 1988) and Pamela M. Eisenbaum, *The Jewish Heroes of Christian History: Hebrews 11 in Literary Context* (SBLDS 156; Atlanta: Scholars Press, 1997).

15. DeSilva mentions passages from both Seneca (*De Beneficiis* 3.36.2–3.38.3) and 4 Macc. (16:16–23) as example lists dealing with similar virtues (*Perseverance* 378–79).

16. In chapter 6.

17. *Perseverance*, 61–62.

18. A good introductory resource on social aspects of the ancient world is Bruce J. Malina's *The New Testament World: Insights from Cultural Anthropology* (Louisville, Ky.: Westminster John Knox, 1993).

19. The notion of "unconditional grace" is thus anachronistic as well.

20. In chapter 6.

21. For an excellent discussion of perfection language in Hebrews, see deSilva, *Perseverance*, 194–204. For an older discussion, see David G. Peterson, *Hebrews and Perfection: An Examination of the Concept of Perfection in the "Epistle to the Hebrews"* (SNTSMS 47; Cambridge: Cambridge University Press, 1982).

22. See chapter 2.

23. For a scholarly treatment of Heb. 12, see N. Clayton Croy's *Endurance in Suffering: Hebrews 12:1–13 in Its Rhetorical, Religious, and Philosophical Context* (SNTSMS 98; Cambridge: Cambridge University Press, 1998).

Chapter 5: A Better Sacrifice, Sanctuary, and Covenant

1. See any of the standard commentaries for the question of whether the word *hilasterion* in Rom. 3:25 refers specifically to the mercy seat on the ark of the covenant (and thus that the verse refers specifically to the Day of Atonement) or is a more general sacrificial metaphor. Many scholars believe this verse echoes an early Christian "hymn."

2. Scholars debate quite vigorously over whether Paul primarily refers to human faith as the key to acceptance by God or *Christ's* faith in passages like Gal. 2:15–21. I do not wish to enter into that debate here. Both positions accept that faith *in* Christ is a crucial element of the equation.

3. However, we can suspect that some of Paul's opponents (perhaps even James and Peter) did not see in Christ's death an end to the Jewish sacrificial system but rather an atonement sufficient enough to cover the past sins of Israel that had kept them from political restoration (cf. 2 Macc. 7:38).

4. For a booklong treatment of the subject, see Susanne Lehne, *The New Covenant in Hebrews* (JSNTSS 44; Sheffield: *JSOT*, 1990).

5. CD 6–7. For this interpretation of the "star" and the "scepter" in this passage, see John J. Collins, *The Star and the Scepter: The Messiahs of the Dead Sea Scrolls and Other Ancient Literature* (New York: Doubleday, 1995), 74–83.

6. Cf. Lehne, *New Covenant*, 26; and Mary R. D'Angelo, *Moses in the Letter to the Hebrews* (SBLDS 42; Missoula, Mont.: Scholars Press, 1979), 243–46. This fact constitutes one of the more significant distinctions between Paul and Hebrews. Paul typically refers to boundary markers between Jew and Gentile in his references to the law (cf. James D. G. Dunn, *Jesus, Paul and the Law: Studies in Mark and Galatians* [Louisville, Ky.: Westminster John Knox, 1990], 191–94); Hebrews to the sacrificial system. The one probable exception to this focus is the more general reference in Heb. 2.2, where the author speaks of the "just punishment" that the law entailed under the old covenant (12:25 similarly).

7. See chapter 2 for some basic information on Philo.

8. See chapter 3 for a more detailed discussion, as well as my article "A Celebration of the Enthroned Son: The Catena of Hebrews 1," *JBL* 120 (2001): 469–85.

9. See chapter 4 for further discussion of Christ and Moses in 3:1–6.

10. The content of Heb. 4:14–16 bears a close resemblance to that of 10:19–24, creating a kind of bracketing effect to the section in between. What makes an analysis of the literary structure of Hebrews difficult is the fact that the author frequently begins themes long before he really discusses them. Furthermore, he often interrupts his train of thought by exhortations that hold the audience's attention.

11. This verse may in fact be the origination of the title "Lord." Perhaps some of the earliest disciples, convinced that Jesus had risen from the dead, found in this verse an explanation for what they had experienced.

12. George W. Buchanan, *To the Hebrews* (Garden City, N.Y.: Doubleday, 1972). While Buchanan's suggestion is tempting, it is in the end unpersuasive. Few have adopted his suggestion.

13. A *metaphor* is the creation of meaning by comparing two unlike things. For example, "he's a sly fox" creates meaning by comparing someone to a fox.

14. For an older summary of the discussion, see Fred L. Horton, *The Melchizedek Tradition: A Critical Examination of the Sources to the Fifth Century A.D. and in the Epistle to the Hebrews* (SNTSMS 30; Cambridge: Cambridge University Press, 1976).

15. A suggestion made by A. S. van der Woude and M. de Jonge, "11Q Melchizedek and the New Testament," *NTS* 12 (1965–66): 301–26.

16. It is for this reason that some have suggested that Melchizedek was a "Christophany"—an appearance of the preexistent Christ in the Old Testament (e.g., Gareth Cockerill, *The Melchizedek Christology in Heb 7:1–28* [Ann Arbor, Mich: University Microfilms International, 1979]). The author, however, nowhere makes such an equation or hints at such a belief. The closest he comes is when he says that Melchizedek is "likened" to the Son of God.

17. In a sense, the exegesis in Heb. 7:1–10 is a *gezerah shewa* argument based on "Melchizedek" as a catchword. The word *Melchizedek* links the text of Ps. 110:4 with Gen. 14.

18. For example, some have seen in it a hymn that predated Hebrews—the height of taking the verse out of context.

19. See chapter 4 for a discussion of perfection in Hebrews. Perfection in this context refers to an actual cleansing of one's sins (cf. Heb. 10:2–3).

20. Hebrews never mentions the Jerusalem temple of Solomon or Herod. Its discussion is strictly theoretical, arguing on the basis of the portable tent the Israelites carried around in their desert wanderings.

21. As we will see in the remainder of the chapter, multiple interpretations exist for a good number of verses in this section. Later in the chapter we will argue for some of the interpretations made here.

22. Some would object to these comments because of a common misunderstanding of the word *metaphor*. It is not uncommon to find people confusing *literal* meanings with *true* meanings. Take the sentence, "He literally went through the roof." What the person should have said was "He *really* went through the roof." To go through the roof literally requires that one's body travel through the ceiling, joists, and out the other side of the roof. To use words literally is to use them in their normal sense.

23. Typical of the metaphorical nature of the author's argument, he mentions Christ's blood in the same breath as the spiritual nature of Christ's offering. The reference to spirit here is often taken to refer to the Holy Spirit, an interpretation I do not think completely contradicts mine. See below for a justification of my emphasis.

24. Hebrews is somewhat unusual in the way it refers to the two chambers of the wilderness sanctuary as the first and second tent.

25. See chapter 2 for a discussion of the meaning of *conscience* in Hebrews.

26. At the very least, the absence of the article indicates that the author is focusing more on the *character* of the sacrifice—spiritual—as opposed to the specific spirit in question.

27. Some would correct my focus on spirit in the afterlife by noting Hebrews's acceptance of the doctrine of resurrection (cf. 6:2), which entailed some sort of continuity with one's body. Even Paul, however, conceptualizes resurrection in terms of a *spiritual* body. I would argue that in the end, Hebrews's argument shows little commitment to the traditional, bodily understanding of resurrection even though he gives it lip service.

28. For a discussion of the various backgrounds suggested for Hebrews, see Lincoln Hurst's *The Epistle to the Hebrews: Its Background of Thought*, SNTSMS 65 (Cambridge: Cambridge University Press, 1990).

29. As n. 20 noted, Hebrews avoids the word *temple* and nowhere makes explicit reference to the Jerusalem temple. Rather, its argument focuses on the portable tent or tabernacle the Israelites used as a sanctuary during the period of their wilderness wanderings. Cf. Acts 7.

30. See my evaluation of this question in "*Philo and the Epistle to the Hebrews*: Ronald Williamson's Study After Thirty Years," *SPhA* 14 (2002): 112–35.

31. The word *hypodeigma*, often mistranslated as "copy," looks similar to the Platonic term *paradeigma*, which in any case means a pattern rather than a copy.

32. I would not deny that much of the language of Heb. 8–10 has a Platonic "feel" to it (especially 10:1). Indeed, I believe Philo's writings provide us with the best single body of background literature for understanding Hebrews's conception of the world, but we have no straightforwardly Platonic argument here.

33. In Hebrews, the plural "holies" generally seems to refer to the Holy of Holies except in 9:2–3, where the distinction between the Holies and the Holy of Holies is made. In 9:8, 12, 24 and 10:19 it seems clear enough that the plural reference to the "holies" alludes to the Holy of Holies.

34. This observation in and of itself does not rule out the "apocalyptic" interpretation, however, since entrance into heaven itself would be a prerequisite to entrance into some heavenly structure.

35. The unusual way in which the author refers to the two chambers of the sanctuary as the "first tent" and "second tent" is one way in which he distances the outer room from that to which the inner room corresponds, namely, heaven itself.

36. This idea is found in both Josephus (*Ant.* 3.180–81) and Philo (*QE* 2.94).

37. For example, Otto Michel, *Der Brief an die Hebräer* (Tübingen: Mohr [Siebeck], 1984), 312.

Chapter 6: The Situation of the Audience

1. The process is, of course, circular. The exegetical decisions we make do feed into our understanding of the audience's situation. On the other hand, our conclusions about the audience's situation also feed back into our interpretations. The question is more one of primacy than exclusivity.

2. This observation presents a significant obstacle to those who propose that the recipients of Hebrews were former Essenes from Qumran. It places the audience most likely into a Hellenistic/Diaspora environment, although Greek was, of course, spoken in Palestine far more than a previous generation of scholars acknowledged.

3. I put the word *Christian* in quotation marks because the author nowhere calls the audience by this title and because of uncertainty regarding whether they were Jews, Gentiles, or a mixture of the two. Jewish Christians in the early church did not think of themselves as converting to Christianity, as if it were a different religion. It was rather true Judaism to them.

4. Although the church settled on Paul as the author of Hebrews from about the fourth century on, it is now practically the unanimous verdict of scholars that Paul was not the author. This fact raises interesting questions about how inspiration and authority work in the words of Scripture, since Hebrews might not have made it into the canon if the church had known Paul was not its writer.

5. Colossians and 1 Peter are often considered pseudonymous. Whatever one's conclusion on this issue, it is significant to note that the secondary names attached to these letters (i.e., besides Paul and Peter) are Timothy and Silas respectively, both of whom were associated with the Pauline mission.

6. Of the "four great unknowns" of the epistle (author, recipients, point of origin, destination), the one answer that has mustered the greatest agreement is the suggestion that Rome is the epistle's destination. At least a significant block of scholars (although probably not a majority) would commit to a Roman audience.

7. Many question the traditional dating of *1 Clement* to around the year 96 C.E. Although we favor a date in the 90s, many now would also allow for the early part of the second century as a possibility.

8. It is also interesting to note that while Hebrews does not appear until the late

second century in any other location (Pantaenus in Alexandria and Tertullian in North Africa), it appears in Rome not only in *1 Clement* but also in the writings of Justin Martyr in the mid-second century. A Roman destination might also shed some light on why, unlike the East, the West hesitated to accept Paul as author until the 300s. Perhaps Roman Christians had a vague recollection that someone else had written it to them.

9. For example, the Roman historian Tacitus notes that Nero not only crucified a number of Christians at that time, but he also had them put on fire to provide light at night and arranged for others to be eaten by animals in sport (*Annals* 15.44).

10. William L. Lane believes that Hebrews was written to Rome between 64 and 68 C.E. and that the previous time of persecution refers to the expulsion of Jewish Christians from Rome during the time of Claudius (ca. 49 C.E., *Hebrews 1–8* [Dallas: Word, 1991], lxiv–lxvi).

11. The Roman historian Suetonius tells us that Claudius expelled Jews from Rome because of disturbances in the Jewish community over "Chrestus," which many scholars think refers to Christ (*Claudius* 25). Acts 18:2 corroborates this expulsion and helps us date it around the year 49 C.E. However, the association of the loss of property in the context of imprisoned Christians (cf. Heb. 10:32–34; 6:10) sounds more like something from Nero's persecution than the expulsion under Claudius.

12. However, we should be careful about putting too much stock in the title "Epistle to the Hebrews." It is reasonable to assume that this title derives from someone second-guessing the epistle's audience on the basis of its content and not because of any real knowledge of its context (e.g., on the basis of Acts 6).

13. David deSilva has also argued that if the foremost element in the situation behind Hebrews is social pressure, the audience's waning faithfulness may not have been a matter of their belief structure but honor/shame considerations (*Perseverance in Gratitude: A Socio-Rhetorical Commentary on the Epistle "to the Hebrews"* [Grand Rapids: Eerdmans, 2000], 5, n. 16).

14. A feature Hebrews shares with 1 Peter, which was written to a Gentile audience (cf. 1 Pet. 2:10).

15. For example, Raymond E. Brown and John P. Meier, *Antioch and Rome: New Testament Cradles of Catholic Christianity* (New York: Paulist, 1983), 110; Joseph A. Fitzmeyer, *Romans* (New York: Doubleday, 1993), 33. The church father Ambrosiaster, writing in Rome about the year 375 C.E., also claimed that the Gentile Roman Christians of the first century had a "Jewish bent" to their Christianity.

16. He sees parallels in the comments about idolatry made in Wis. 13:10, 18; 15:5, 17 (*Perseverance*, 2–7; 216–17).

17. For example, Clement indicates that Peter and Paul lost their lives to Nero because of "jealousy" (*1 Clem.* 5). While we cannot know for certain whose jealousy Clement means, mainstream Jews in Rome are a strong option. The incident during the reign of Claudius probably indicates that significant tension could arise among the synagogues in Rome over Christ (see n. 12 above).

18. For example, Tacitus, *Annals* 14.44; Suetonius, *Nero* 16.

19. See, for example, L. L. Thompson, *The Book of Revelation: Apocalypse and Empire* (New York: Oxford University Press, 1990).

20. *Roman History* 67.14.1.

21. Indeed, if some rather well connected individuals were a part of Hebrews's audience, the image of Moses' choice of God over the house of Pharaoh would make the rhetoric of Heb. 11 especially poignant. The author would implicitly urge

such persons to suffer with the people of God rather than enjoy the treasures of "Egypt." He would encourage those facing exile not to fear "the anger of the king." Glabrio's name in particular is associated with some of the Christian catacombs from this period.

22. For example, Suetonius, *Domitian* 13.
23. For example, Rev. 13, which may in fact portray Domitian figuratively as Nero come back from the dead.
24. Raymond E. Brown, *An Introduction to the New Testament* (New York: Doubleday, 1997), 805–9 gives an excellent list of ancient witnesses to at least a limited persecution of Christians under Domitian.
25. In a well-known passage from Ovid's writings, for example, the Roman poet begs for Augustus to allow him to come to a location closer to Rome than he is (*Tristia* 2.179–91).
26. Could these be the "aliens and strangers" to whom 1 Peter is addressed (1 Pet. 2:11), individuals from the Roman church exiled to Pontus, Galatia, Cappadocia, Asia, and Bithynia (1:1) during the reign of Domitian?
27. Cf. Suetonius, *Domitian* 12, where Domitian prosecutes some who "lived as Jews" without publicly acknowledging Judaism as their religion. Could these be Christians?
28. The question of "second repentance"—whether a Christian can find forgiveness for his or her sins more than once—is an issue that surfaced in the early church particularly when Christians betrayed Christ by offering sacrifices to the emperor and the gods. Clement seems to contradict Hebrews intentionally when he says that "in generation after generation the master has given a *place of repentance* to those wishing to return to him" (*1 Clem* 7.5; contrast Heb. 12:17 where Esau cannot find a "place of repentance"). The Shepherd of Hermas wrestles with the same issue in the second century, allowing that all the sins of Christians up to that point could be forgiven. In contrast, those who apostasized in the coming crisis would not have another chance at forgiveness (Herm. *Vis.* 2.2.4–5).
29. Cf. Josephus, *Ant.* 14.227.
30. Cf. Josephus, *Ant.* 14.214 for clear evidence of the communal meals celebrated by the Jews in the Diaspora.
31. *Patrologia Latina* 17.46.
32. Notice that the author of Acts even has Paul offer a sacrifice in Jerusalem (Acts 21:24, 26).
33. Cassius Dio, *Roman History* 67.14.1.
34. *De superstitione*, quoted by Augustine in *The City of God* 6.11 (quotation taken from the Loeb translation).
35. Eusebius, *HE* 6.25.13.

Glossary

atonement: The reconciliation of humanity to God made by way of sacrifice or some offering in order to make amends.

chiasm: A literary device that functions on an A B B' A' pattern. The first and last lines correspond to each other, as do the B and B' lines. It is possible to have an infinite number of other corresponding lines (e.g., C and C').

Christology: The study of the person of Christ.

Day of Atonement: Yom Kippur, the one day a year when the high priest entered into the innermost room of the sanctuary (the Holy of Holies or Most Holy Place). The high priest atoned for all the sins of the people on this day (cf. Lev. 16; Num. 29).

discourse: The words on the page of a text—a text as it presents itself to a reader.

events: The things that take place in a story.

exhortation: A genre whose primary orientation is toward moving the audience to take a course of action.

exposition: A genre whose primary orientation is toward deriving truths from the interpretation of Scripture.

faith: In Hebrews, enduring in faithfulness because one trusts in what God has promised without visible evidence that it is going to come true.

gezerah shewa: A Jewish interpretive method that interprets one scriptural text by linking it with another text that uses similar words.

Hellenistic: Greek in culture or Greek speaking.

homily: A short sermon.

inclusio: A way of binding a section of text together by beginning and ending it with similar words, phrases, or ideas.

Life of Adam and Eve: Known mainly from its later Christian form, an earlier Hebrew version may have dated from the first century C.E. It imaginatively fills in missing details from the Genesis story of Adam and Eve's "fall."

Middle Platonism: A philosophical tradition that developed from the merging of Platonic and Stoic ideas in the late-first-century B.C.E. Like Middle Stoicism, it held that the human spirit derived from the divine Word or *logos* that directed the world. Like Platonism, it believed that the material world was a copy of heavenly patterns, which it equated with the Stoic *logos*.

narrative: Story, in form or nature.

narrative criticism: An approach to interpretation that "brackets" historical factors as much as possible in order to read a story as a self-contained world.

non in thora non in mundo: A Jewish exegetical technique based on the idea that if the Torah was silent about something, then that thing could be considered not to exist for interpretive purposes.

parousia: The arrival of Christ on earth from heaven on the day of judgment.

patron-client relationships: Informal arrangements by which those with resources (patrons) supplied those without (clients) in return for the honor and prestige they gained. In between the two parties often stood brokers that mediated such resources.

perfection (Christ): Relates to Christ's successful, sinless completion of the human experience and the subsequent attainment of glory as he is exalted to God's right hand.

perfection (human): In Hebrews, relates to the cleansing of sins and the consequent attainment of glory in the heavenly realm.

Philo: A Jewish interpreter of the Hebrew Scriptures who lived in the Egyptian city of Alexandria during the time of Christ. He drew heavily on Middle Platonic categories for his interpretations.

plot: The combination of events, characters, and settings such that they comprise a story.

qal wohomer: Literally "light and heavy," an exegetical technique that argues that if something is true of a lesser example, then it is certainly true of a greater one.

rhetoric: Words formulated in such a way as to persuade.

salvation history: The story of how God has brought salvation to his people.

Septuagint: Technically the Greek translation of the Pentateuch, the term is often used of the entirety of the Greek Old Testament used by Christians at the time of Christ.

settings: The times and places where things happen in a story.

sin offering: One of the five basic offerings prescribed by Leviticus (Lev. 4), its purpose was to provide atonement for unintentional sins one might commit (sins committed in ignorance).

story world: The abstracted story—with events, characters, and settings—that is evoked by a text. Such a text might be a narrative version of the story (the same story can be narrated in many different ways) or some other kind of "text," like a sermon making an argument from a story.

tradition history: The way a particular term, concept, or Scripture was used and developed in the history of a tradition such as early Christianity.

Wisdom of Solomon: A book of wisdom reputed to come from Solomon, written in Alexandria either the first century before or after Christ. It reflects the influence of Middle Platonism at various points.

Bibliography

Selected Commentaries

Attridge, Harold W. *The Epistle to the Hebrews: A Commentary on the Epistle to the Hebrews*. Philadelphia: Fortress, 1989.

Buchanan, George W. *To the Hebrews*. Garden City, N.Y.: Doubleday, 1972.

deSilva, David A. *Perseverance in Gratitude: A Socio-Rhetorical Commentary on the Epistle "to the Hebrews."* Grand Rapids: Eerdmans, 2000.

Ellingworth, Paul. *The Epistle to the Hebrews*. Grand Rapids: Eerdmans, 1993.

Guthrie, George H. *Hebrews*. Grand Rapids: Zondervan, 1998.

Hagner, Donald A. *Hebrews*. Peabody, Mass: Hendrickson, 1990.

Hughes, Philip E. *A Commentary on the Epistle to the Hebrews*. Grand Rapids: Eerdmans, 1977.

Koester, Craig R. *Hebrews: A New Translation with Introduction and Commentary*. New York: Doubleday, 2001.

Lane, William L. *Hebrews*. 2 vols. Dallas: Word, 1991.

Michel, Otto. *Der Brief an die Hebräer*. Tübingen: Mohr [Siebeck], 1984.

Selected Monographs and Articles

Attridge, Harold W. "'Heard Because of His Reverence' (Heb 5:7)." *JBL* 98 (1979): 90–93.

Barrett, C. K. "The Eschatology of the Epistle to the Hebrews," in *The Background of the New Testament and Its Eschatology: Studies in Honour of C. H. Dodd*. Cambridge: Cambridge University Press, 1964, 363–93.

Beker, J. Christiaan. *Paul the Apostle: The Triumph of God in Life and Thought*. Edinburgh: T & T Clark, 1980.

Brooks, Walter E. "The Perpetuity of Christ's Sacrifice in the Epistle to the Hebrews." *JBL* 89 (1970): 205–14.

Brown, Raymond E. and Meier, John P. *Antioch and Rome: New Testament Cradles of Catholic Christianity*. New York: Paulist, 1983.

Caird, G. B. "The Exegetical Method of the Epistle to the Hebrews." *CJT* 5 (1959): 44–51.

Cockerill, Gareth. *The Melchizedek Christology in Heb. 7:1–28*. Ann Arbor, Mich.: University Microfilms International, 1979.

Collins, John J. *The Star and the Scepter: The Messiahs of the Dead Sea Scrolls and Other Ancient Literature*. New York: Doubleday, 1995.

Cosby, Michael R. *The Rhetorical Composition and Function of Hebrews 11: In Light of Example Lists of Antiquity*. Macon, Ga.: Mercer University Press, 1988.

Croy, N. Clayton. *Endurance in Suffering: Hebrews 12:1–13 in Its Rhetorical, Religious, and Philosophical Context*. SNTSMS 98; Cambridge: Cambridge University Press, 1998.

D'Angelo, Mary R. *Moses in the Letter to the Hebrews*. SBLDS 42; Missoula Mont.: Scholars Press, 1979.

deSilva, David A. *Despising Shame: Honor Discourse and Community Maintenance in the Epistle to the Hebrews*. SBLDS 152; Atlanta: Scholars Press, 1995.

Dunn, James D. G. *Jesus, Paul and the Law: Studies in Mark and Galatians*. Louisville, Ky.: Westminster John Knox, 1990.

Eisenbaum, Pamela M. *The Jewish Heroes of Christian History: Hebrews 11 in Literary Context*. SBLDS 156; Atlanta: Scholars Press, 1997.

Fitzmyer, Joseph A. *Romans*. New York: Doubleday, 1993.

_____. "A Feature of Qumran Angelology and the Angels of I Cor 11:10," *NTS* 4 (1957–58): 48–58.

Guthrie, George H. *The Structure of Hebrews: A Text-Linguistic Analysis*. SNT 73; Leiden: E. J. Brill, 1994.

Hay, David M. *Glory at the Right Hand: Ps 110:1 in Early Christianity*. SBLDS 18; Nashville: Abingdon, 1973.

Hays, Richard B. "Christ Prays the Psalms: Paul's Use of an Early Christian Exegetical Convention," in *The Future of Christology: Essays in Honor of Leander E. Keck*. Minneapolis: Fortress, 1993, 122–36.

_____. *The Faith of Jesus Christ*. Chico, Calif.: Scholars Press, 1983.

Horton, Fred L. *The Melchizedek Tradition: A Critical Examination of the Sources to the Fifth Century A.D. and in the Epistle to the Hebrews*. SNTSMS 30; Cambridge: Cambridge University Press, 1976.

Hurst, Lincoln. *The Epistle to the Hebrews: Its Background of Thought*. SNTSMS 65; Cambridge: Cambridge University Press, 1990.

_____. "The Christology of Heb 1 and 2," in *The Glory of Christ in the New Testament: Studies in Christology in Memory of George Bradford Caird*. Eds. L. D. Hurst and N. T. Wright. Oxford: Clarendon, 1987, 151–64.

_____. "How 'Platonic' Are Heb. viii.5 and ix.23f?," *JTS* 34 (1983): 156–68.

Käsemann, Ernst. *The Wandering People of God: An Investigation of the Letter to the Hebrews*. Minneapolis: Augsburg, 1984 [1957].

Kistemaker, Simon J. *The Psalm Citations in the Epistle to the Hebrews*. Amsterdam: Van Soest, 1961.

Lehne, Susanne. *The New Covenant in Hebrews*. JSNTSS 44; Sheffield: JSOT, 1990.

Longenecker, Richard N. *Biblical Exegesis in the Apostolic Period*. Grand Rapids: Eerdmans, 1975.

Malina, Bruce J. *The New Testament World: Insights from Cultural Anthropology*. Louisville, Ky.: Westminster John Knox, 1993.

Martin, Dale B. *The Corinthian Body*. New Haven, Conn.: Yale University Press, 1995.

Meier, John P. "Structure and Theology in Heb 1,1–4," *Bib* 66 (1985): 168–89.

_____. "Symmetry and Theology in Heb 1,5–14," *Bib* 66 (1985): 504–33.

Moore, Stephen. *Literary Criticism and the Gospels: The Theoretical Challenge*. New Haven, Conn.: Yale University Press, 1989.

Mowinckel, Sigmund. *The Psalms in Israel's Worship*. Oxford: Oxford University Press, 1962.

Patte, Daniel. *What Is Structural Exegesis?* Philadelphia: Fortress, 1976.

Petersen, Norman R. *Rediscovering Paul: Philemon and the Sociology of Paul's Narrative World.* Philadelphia: Fortress, 1985.

Peterson, David G. *Hebrews and Perfection: An Examination of the Concept of Perfection in the "Epistle to the Hebrews."* Cambridge: Cambridge University Press, 1982.

Powell, Mark A. *What Is Narrative Criticism?* Minneapolis: Fortress, 1990.

Schenck, Kenneth L. "*Philo and the Epistle to the Hebrews*: Ronald Williamson's Study After Thirty Years." *SPhA* 14 (2002): 112–35.

_____. "The Celebration of the Enthroned Son: The Catena of Hebrews 1:5–14." *JBL* 120 (2001): 469–85.

_____. "Keeping His Appointment: Creation and Enthronement in the Epistle to the Hebrews." *JSNT* 66 (1996): 91–117.

Stott, Wilfrid. "The Conception of 'Offering' in the Epistle to the Hebrews." *NTS* 9 (1962–63): 62–67.

Stuckenbruck, Loren T. *Angel Veneration and Christology: A Study in Early Judaism and in the Christology of the Apocalypse of John.* WUNT 70; Tübingen: Mohr [Siebeck], 1995.

Thompson, James W. *The Beginnings of Christian Philosophy: The Epistle to the Hebrews.* CBQMS 13; Washington, D.C.: Catholic Biblical Association, 1982.

Thompson, L. L. *The Book of Revelation: Apocalypse and Empire.* New York: Oxford University Press, 1990.

van der Woude, A. S. and de Jonge, M. "11Q Melchizedek and the New Testament." *NTS* 12 (1965–66): 301–26.

Witherington, Ben III. *Paul's Narrative Thought World: The Tapestry of Tragedy and Triumph.* Louisville, Ky.: Westminster John Knox, 1994.

Wright, N. T. *The New Testament and the People of God.* Minneapolis: Fortress, 1992.

Scripture and Ancient Source Index

Scholar Index

Subject Index